D0840306

LOOKING AT
Edward Bawden and Great Bardfield
LIFE IN AN ENGLISH VILLAGE

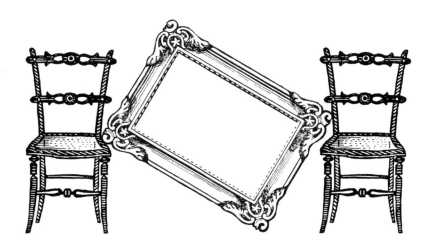

LOOKING AT

Edward Bawden and Great Bardfield

LIFE IN AN ENGLISH VILLAGE

CAMBRIDGE

First Published 2022.
Inexpensive Progress, Cambridge, UK.
www.inexpensiveprogress.com

10 9 8 7 6 5 4 3 2 1
ISBN: 978-1-7391-6600-7

All rights reserved. No part of this publication may be reproduced, distributed, or transmitted in any form or by any means, or stored in a retrieval system or transmitted in any form or by any means, electronic, mechanical, photo-copying, recording or otherwise, without permission of the publisher.

The rights of Robjn Cantus to be identified as the author of this work have been asserted by him in accordance with the Copyright, Designs and Patents Act 1988. The moral right of the author(s) has been asserted. Every effort has been made to seek permission to reproduce images. A catalogue record for this book is available within the British Library.

Text, research and commentary by Robjn Cantus.
Additional research by Stella Herbert.
Designed by Inexpensive Progress.
Typeset in Adobe Jenson Pro.
Edited by Alex Schultz.
Printed by Swallowtail Print, Norwich.

Thanks to:
Alex Schultz, Stella Herbert, Tim Mainstone, Penguin Books, the Edward Bawden Estate, the Fry Art Gallery, the Higgins Bedford, Alan Pritt, Chloe Cheese, David Herbert, Colin Wilkin, Victoria Partridge, Helen Brown, Gordon Cummings, Richard & Hattie Bawden, Louise Bawden, Silas Clifford-Smith, Sheila Aldridge, Caroline Aldridge, Denise Hoyle, Nina Hoyle, Michael and Lucy Archer and Neil Jennings.

CONTENTS

7   FOREWORD BY CHLOE CHEESE

9   INTRODUCTION

23   NOEL CARRINGTON

29   EDWARD BAWDEN

37   KING PENGUIN BOOKS

43   THE PRINTING

47   THE ILLUSTRATIONS

123   THE ARTISTS' LIVES

145   AFTER THE WAR

151   NOT FORGOTTEN

157   AN INTERVIEW WITH EDWARD BAWDEN BY MARTIN GAYFORD, from *Modern Painters*, 1989

169   BIBLIOGRAPHY

171   IMAGE REFERENCES

CHLOE CHEESE - GREAT BARDFIELD CAT, 2010

FOREWORD

Robjn Cantus knows Great Bardfield well. He has centred his writing on Great Bardfield around *Life in an English Village*, published in 1949 and so well illustrated with Edward Bawden's drawings of everyday village life.

I first went to live in Great Bardfield as a small child about seven years after *Life in an English Village* was published, when things were beginning to change but much was still recognisable from Edward's images, which are affectionate but also truthful. (I attended the village school, which was still as shown.)

Each person who writes about Great Bardfield brings something new or a different angle I had not reflected on before, and I find that the more people write about Great Bardfield the more it is possible to understand this rather odd collection of artists who imposed themselves upon a traditional Essex village then undergoing the changes brought about in all rural farming communities after the two world wars. Reading about the history of the village and houses makes the context for the villagers and artists more lively.

The artists lived their own lives but were still aware and observant of the life around them. Some of their work depicting the village can look nostalgic now, but it is a record of what was there. Edward Bawden in particular – who was a native of Essex, although he travelled extensively – felt a sense of belonging in the village and its surrounding landscape.

I hope the families of villagers portrayed in this book still enjoy having part of their past serve as a lasting record for us all to enjoy.

CHLOE CHEESE

EDWARD BAWDEN - THE ROAD TO THAXTED, 1956

INTRODUCTION

"The village which I have had in mind all along is these pages is the agricultural village."
NOEL CARRINGTON · LIFE IN AN ENGLISH VILLAGE

The ancient county of Essex has a great deal of industry on its southern borders, nearer London and following the River Thames, but the farther north you get, the more rural it becomes. As in most of Great Britain, the landscape is man-made, with many of the giant woodlands, used for hunting game eight hundred years ago, cut down, long ago and the land given over to farming. Agriculture is at the heart of the formation of Essex, and the villages on the maps are linked to the farms and rivers throughout the landscape. What to us is a village would have been considered a town before the Industrial Revolution, but the population of these settlements would always have been in flux, and the presence of migratory workers at certain times of the year to tend to hops and crops and manually bring in the harvest would temporarily cause a settlement to grow. Fortunes depended on trade, and the small markets in the village centres can still be seen, now used as the 'green', bounded by a triangle of roads. These would be populated by local sellers and travelling merchants with carts. The village buildings around the green were originally thatched timber-framed shops or inns, which were later faced with bricks, depending on the wealth of the area.

As a rural village, Great Bardfield had a thriving market and was known for spinning wool and producing cloth. Located on one of the main roads into London, it had a sizable market in 1224, having gained in size to become of note. Here produce and cloth were traded for wool and food bought by the locals. Farming was for centuries one of the biggest industries, and many halls and manor houses survive from the Tudor period.

Even after serfdom had fully ended, in 1574, the people of a village generally remained economically tied to large estates. The cottages that up to the nineteenth century would have been on the fringes of the village were housing for farming workers. These were then small dwellings; the luxury of additional space could not be justified, and only as a family grew in size might extensions and modifications be made, normally by craftsmen without the aid of an architect. Comfort wasn't a priority.

A beautiful village can not be designed or forced into existence. Architectural elements must be left to chance and the myriad of choices people will make over centuries: for thatched, tiled or slate roofs, for white or red brick, for plastered or pargetted walls. The history of domestic architecture is a tricky one to pin down, but the Greek for *architect* translates as 'chief carpenter', and it really was a craft of the builder. The Royal Institute of British Architects was only established in 1834, to try to standardise building practices with law. Local merchants would know where to acquire stone, pipes and timber, and these were normally in keeping with the local architectural vernacular.

As big estates were broken up into smaller farms, and as mechanisation reduced the number of men needed on the land, workers' cottages were sold, typically with some land to be farmed. These small holdings became an important way of life for villagers, who would grow flowers or food for themselves or for extra income. In the twentieth century this land would in turn be sold for building, and the infilled cottages dotted over the old homesteads appear today to be part of the main village.

ABOVE AND BELOW: OPPOSITE ENDS OF THE HIGH STREET, GREAT BARDFIELD

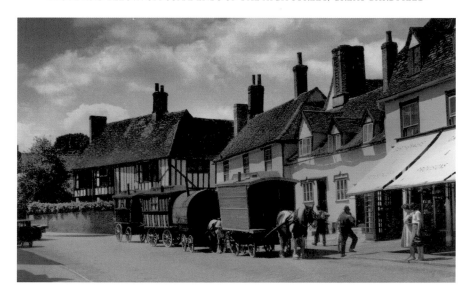

ABOVE: SHEILA ROBINSON - BROOK STREET, GREAT BARDFIELD. BELOW: AN OLD HAND-TINTED PHOTO

"As the life of the village changes, so must its physical appearance. It cannot remain for the benefit of the tourist a shell of its vanished social life."
NOEL CARRINGTON · LIFE IN AN ENGLISH VILLAGE

For many people a village is a place unspoilt by the city and off the main roads, with a small school, footpaths over fields and dominated by a church with a series of pubs in the centre at the junction of old roads.

Located above Braintree, in north Essex, Great Bardfield has retained most of the charm of a village, though much of its local commerce has departed. The small food shops have largely been replaced by one Co-op, and the tailor and forge are long gone, but it still has the feel of a living village, in contrast to the centre of nearby Lavenham, which has been frozen by the architectural constraints imposed to protect its beautiful buildings. The villagers today are aware of Great Bardfield's continued beauty and artistic legacy, as is apparent in the local bookshop and the Cottage Museum.

The pubs are popular with groups of cyclists making use of the country roads from London, while motorcyclists congregate in the nearby beauty spot of Finchingfield.

In the 1940s a village might still have had a saddle maker's, shops for dry, tinned and hardware goods, as well as a butcher's shop, mill and baker. In 1949, when *Life in an English Village* was published, Britain was recovering from the Second World War. The pound had been devalued by the government to boost British exports and welcome foreign money into the economy. Although the victors in the war, Britain's presence in the world was shaken when in 1947 India gained independence and in 1948 the British left Palestine.

Although sweet and clothing rationing ended in 1949, food rationing for meat and basic

ABOVE: FARMING IN GREAT BARDFIELD. BELOW: THE CORONATION OF THE KING

produce continued until 1954. The 1950s was a decade of rapid innovation in the home, but at the time of *Life in an English Village* traditional techniques were still in practice and automation was yet to be seen everywhere in the countryside.

Many people in Great Bardfield didn't own a car in the 1930s and '40s, relying on London Transport's Green Line bus service or bicycles to get to the capital or the nearest railway station. Great Bardfield was surrounded by various railway routes in the 1940s, all part of the London and North Eastern Railway service, allowing locals to drive or go by bus to the most convenient station for their destination: from Braintree (to Colchester, Chelmsford, London), Thaxted (London, Cambridge) or Sible and Castle Hedingham (Cambridge, Colchester). Many of these lines were axed when railway services were cut back following Dr Beeching's 1963 report *The Reshaping of British Railways*. By this time, car ownership was becoming more affordable and some even argue that the closure of so many branch-line railway routes helped protect the countryside by making it less accessible. Though much of this sounds somewhat gloomy, working and social conditions were due for change, and just as the First World War paved the way for women getting the vote, the Second World War helped shake off some social constraints that had persisted into the 1930s.

The local newspaper in 1949 has something rather nostalgic about it when it reports on the Great Bardfield village fete, flower show and sports day held on the August bank holiday and opened by local gentry, Sir John Archibald Ruggles-Brise, who was living at Spains Hall, on the edge of Great Bardfield (now home to the chef Jamie Oliver). At this fete the band of the Essex Regiment regaled the crowds; teas, light refreshments and ices were served; prizes were given for the flowers and winning sports teams. It was still the England people now memorialise.

Great Bardfield even had its own whist team; they competed against other villages in the area and the prizes were all to be useful to the community. At one competition, the Bardfield team won new crockery for the town hall and the Wethersfield team won mops and dusters for their village hall.

Like so many villages in the area, Great Bardfield has a chain of namesakes: Bardfield End Green, Little Bardfield, Bardfield Saling, though locally these were collectively known as the 'fields', with Wethersfield and Finchingfield included with the various Bardfields.

For a long time, a successful annual horse fair was held in Great Bardfield, but by around the time of the First World War the event was in decline as British agriculture became more mechanised. Steam-powered threshing machines, run by a larger machine such as a traction engine, would have been the first innovation for hundreds of years on the farm in the late nineteenth century. The next innovations after the First World War were tractors and other machines powered by diesel-fuelled internal combustion engines. Diesel engines also gave rise to trucks that could transport crops.

Edward Bawden would have been made familiar with what was happening in farming by his friend Thomas Hennell, whom he met in the kitchen of Bawden's home, Brick House, in 1931, when Hennell rented a room there for the night. Hennell was cycling around the county researching and illustrating his book *Change in the Farm* (1934). Bawden and Tirzah Ravilious both noted that Hennell had a corn dolly attached to his bike, as Hennell was collecting memories of all things rural before they were lost. As Hennell wrote in the introduction to his book, "In every farmyard,

THOMAS HENNELL - FLAIL THRESHING, 1944

EDWARD BAWDEN · GREAT LODGE BARN, GREAT BARDFIELD · FROM A ZINC ADVERTISMENT, 1945

outhouse and contingent building throughout the country are to be seen piled-up relics of past generations of farmers – the remains of old ploughs, wagons and implements crumbling away behind the new steam-thresher and brightly-painted iron rakes and harrows." Many of these rubbish dumps of old machinery were favourite subjects of Bawden and Eric Ravilious in the 1930s. The First World War had taken a toll on all industries in Britain, as so many men had died, and machines were welcomed to share the work. By the time of *Life in an English Village* a great deal of machinery was in use on the farms, but it remained limited to ploughs and other items that could be attached to a tractor, and many farms still had horses and employed villagers on the land.

The 1949 King Penguin book *Life in an English Village*, with an introduction by Noel Carrington, was proposed and illustrated by Edward Bawden. With such a topic, Bawden looked to his own village for his source material – places like the bakery and the butcher shop and the people who worked in them – and the illustrations amount to a visual biography of Great Bardfield and its inhabitants, though nowhere in the text by Carrington does he mention what village is being depicted.

The volume closely followed Bawden's other

publication as an illustrator for Penguin Books, *The Arabs* (1947), with an essay by R.B. Serjeant. In *The Arabs*, which appeared under the publisher's Puffin children's book imprint, Bawden used his portraits and paintings of real people and places from his time as a war artist to make the work as accurate as possible. *Life in an English Village* allowed him to put those journalistic skills to use in peacetime.

The illustrations in *Life in an English Village* have two striking qualities. First, Bawden was known at the time as a landscape painter, and all the views are interiors, underlining that the life of an English village is its people. The second is that the illustrations all depict someone quietly and intently focused on a job – the vicar writing at his desk, women cleaning the church and the Methodist chapel – in stark contrast to the turmoil of the war of the recent past.

This human presence also helps give the interiors life, far from being a National Trust series of picturesque empty properties, these interiors are all occupied and used.

Today people might think the artists ran the village of Great Bardfield, but other than Charlotte Bawden, who was president of the Bardfield Women's Institute, most of them were too busy to join in the running of committees, charity collections, the parish council and the like. And there were a few families whose names pop up in the newspapers from the period over and again, as well as in the church's graveyard: the Hitchcocks, the Daveys, the Crossmans and the Piper family, who ran various businesses in the village.

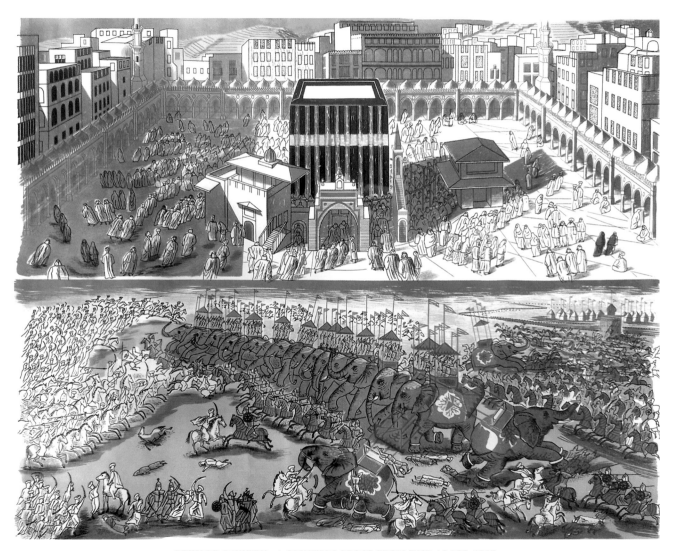

EDWARD BAWDEN - A PRINTERS PROOF FROM THE ARABS, 1947

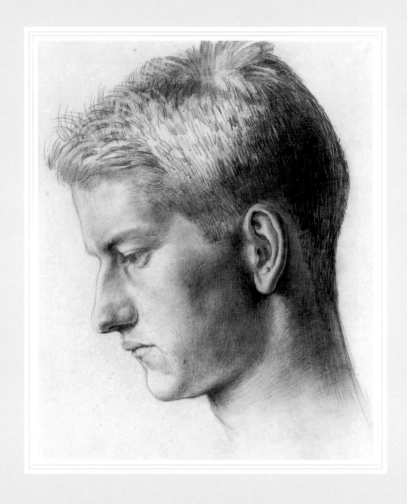

DORA CARRINGTON · NOEL CARRINGTON, 1918

NOEL CARRINGTON

Noel Carrington is less well known today than he ought to be. He is most famous now for being the brother of Dora Carrington, who herself is remembered better for her famous relationships with Mark Gertler and Lytton Strachey than for her paintings. A student at the Slade School of Art from 1910 to 1914, Dora did bring Noel into contact with her fellow students (Paul Nash, C.R.W. Nevinson and Stanley Spencer among them), many of them to become his lifelong friends. In return Noel introduced Dora to his fellow Oxonian Ralph Partridge, whom Dora later married. Noel and Dora were raised in Bedford with their siblings Sam, Teddy and Charlotte. Their father, Samuel, had worked for the East Indian Railway. Their mother, Charlotte Houghton, had been a governess. Noel described their childhood as "uneventful and certainly not unhappy". He was educated in Oxford and rowed for his college.

Carrington served in the First World War and was wounded in his right elbow. After the war he returned to Oxford, but instead of continuing his education he joined the Oxford University Press (OUP). In 1919 he followed in his father's footsteps when he went to India, to replace the ailing E.V. Rieu in the Bombay office of the OUP. The following year, Carrington was offered the chance to set up a new branch of the press in Calcutta. The OUP had started on a wave of bringing popular books on Indian and Asian philosophy to the West, while also printing and publishing educational books for the British government in India, and while in India Carrington learnt the book publishing trade and worked hands-on with printers.

Carrington returned to Britain in 1923, and in 1925 he married Catherine Alexander

(1904–2004), a Slade School artist, who was the daughter of his next-door neighbour Philip Alexander. Philip was a member of the Design and Industries Association, which had members from across London's top companies and publishing firms and had a broad effect on printing and society. In 1930 the association printed its yearbook *The Face of the Land* and in the introduction stated, "Our aim, in compiling this book, has been to stimulate public interest in a very vital matter, namely the beauty of our country and the seemliness of our civilisation." The book makes the case that the countryside should be protected, that the building of rural houses should be in keeping with local styles and that advertising such as hoardings and enamel signs be removed from buildings. These concerns about conservation and craft stayed with Carrington and his awareness of the countryside is noted in his essay for *Life in an English Village*.

In the 1930s Carrington started to work for the Kynoch Press, based in Birmingham. It was a strange satellite unit, a printing wing of the Kynoch ammunitions company. The company produced an annual calendar and each year it was illustrated by a different artist. Eric Ravilious was hired to work on the 1933 *Kynoch Press Note Book*, and Edward Bawden illustrated the 1935 edition. The press also took on printing work for others and in 1933 produced *Broadway and the Cotswolds*, a local guide published for the Lygon Arms hotel, with text by Carrington and a wood engraving by Ravilious on the cover depicting the Lygon Arms.

From the mid-1920s Carrington worked for *Country Life* in their book publishing department, leaving in 1928 and returning to work for them again from 1935 to 1940. In this later phase it seems he gained considerably more influence over what could be published, and he helped publish Kathleen Hale's first Orlando

ERIC RAVILIOUS - VIGNETTES FOR MAY AND OCTOBER,
FROM THE COUNTRY LIFE COOKERY BOOK, 1937

book, as well as *The Country Life Cookery Book* (1937) and *High Street* (1938), both illustrated by Ravilious.

Carrington's next adventure in the book trade came when he suggested to Allen Lane of Penguin Books a line of colourful and cheap books for children. This resulted in the Puffin Books imprint, most of which, in the early days, were illustrated educational books, though a dozen or so were fiction. Penguin had wanted to get into children's publishing for some time but needed someone with Carrington's technical ability to make it happen. It is quite likely Carrington and Lane had both read an article in the January 1934 issue of *Design for To-Day* by Pearl Binder on Russian children's books of the 1920s and '30s.

After editing a large number of Puffin picture books, Carrington then joined the government industry and design boards. He was replaced at Puffin by Eleanor Graham and then Kaye Webb, who would keep the imprint up to date with changing trends in design.

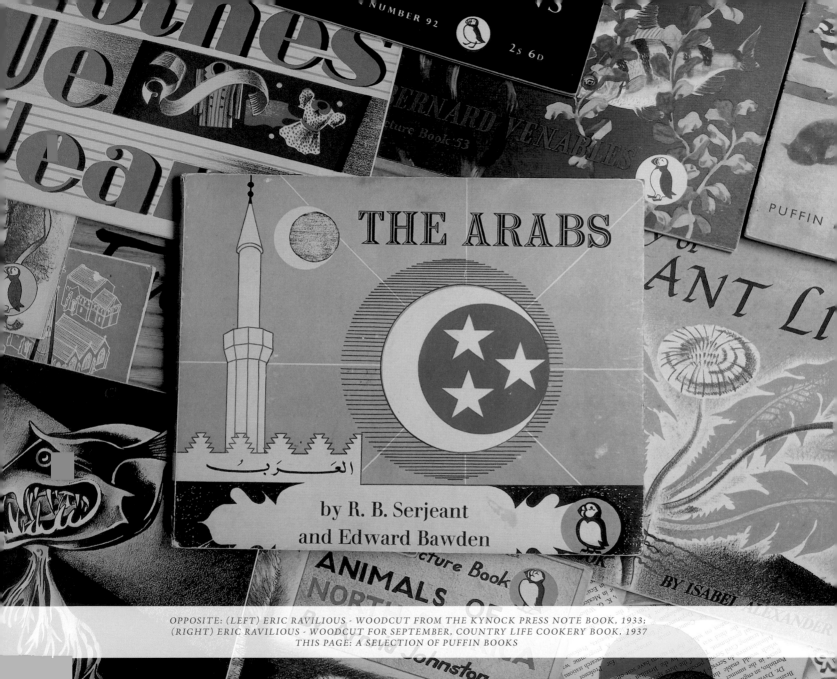

THE ARABS

العَرَب

by R. B. Serjeant
and Edward Bawden

OPPOSITE: (LEFT) ERIC RAVILIOUS - WOODCUT FROM THE KYNOCK PRESS NOTE BOOK, 1933;
(RIGHT) ERIC RAVILIOUS - WOODCUT FOR SEPTEMBER, COUNTRY LIFE COOKERY BOOK, 1937
THIS PAGE: A SELECTION OF PUFFIN BOOKS

DAVID EVAN EDWARDS - EDWARD BAWDEN, 1974

EDWARD BAWDEN

Edward Bawden was born in Braintree, Essex, in 1903. The son of an ironmonger, he never had any plans or desire to take up the family trade, and in fact illness helped determine what he would do in life. Bawden claimed that at thirteen he strained his heart swimming. In his weakened condition, "good at nothing", he spent his time "copying from magazines like *The Girl's Own Paper* and Louis Wain's cats, and that sort of thing", he told an interviewer in 1984. When he showed little interest in anything formal education had to offer, his school agreed that he could have one lesson every week at the Cambridge School of Art to see if that would motivate him, and it did. He stayed on at Cambridge and then, in 1922, went to the Royal College of Art, where he was introduced to the work of Edward Lear and Richard 'Dickie' Doyle. These illustrators changed his approach forever.

Before the Royal College of Art (RCA), Bawden had never had the opportunity to see anything like the work of Lear or Doyle. "Where could you discover anything in Braintree around 1914?" he told Martin Gayford in 1989. At the RCA, Bawden entered a large pool of talented students, among them Douglas Percy Bliss, Eric Ravilious, Enid Marx, Barnett Freedman, Percy Horton, Peggy Angus, Norah Braden and Charlotte Epton. This period in the interwar years is seen as a golden era at the college. Bawden entered the RCA's design school for training in what now would be called graphic design and illustration. The college's professor of design was Robert Anning Bell, known mostly for his stained glass and book illustration. The principal of the school was William Rothenstein, who invited Paul Nash to teach in the design school for two terms. Nash later reflected that his pupils Marx, Bawden, Ravilious and others were an "outbreak of talent". After Bawden met Ravilious, also in his first year at the college, they became good friends. They were an odd pairing: Bawden was known to be shy and fastidious; Ravilious in contrast was confident and enthusiastic.

Of all the artists of Great Bardfield, it is Ravilious and Bawden whose lives have been most documented, with recent major London exhibitions on each. After completing their studies at the RCA, Bawden and Ravilious lodged in houses in London, but both wanted a place in the countryside to retreat to from the city. In 1925, cycling around the Braintree area, they came across Brick House in Great Bardfield, where they rented rooms from Mrs Kinnear.

Eric had taken up teaching part time at Eastbourne School of Art, and he started to date one of his pupils, the wood engraver and painter Tirzah Garwood. In 1930 they were married.

History could have taken very different turn in that summer, when, on a visit to the writer A.J.A. Symons, in the neighbouring village and beauty spot of Finchingfield, Bawden chanced upon a house and barn up for rent. He wrote "a pro-Essex campaign to Eric & Tirzah Ravilious, Barnett and Claudia Freedman, Bowk [Beryl Bowker] & Robert Sinclair", suggesting they all rent the property together in a commune. It would have been like taking that

High Street, Bardfield   140237

generation of Royal College of Art graduates and tipping it into an Essex house, but with limited enthusiasm from the others it didn't come to pass.

In 1932 Bawden married his RCA friend Charlotte Epton. After leaving the art school Charlotte had worked at Bernard Leach's new pottery in St Ives while learning more about the technical elements of the craft. As a wedding gift, Bawden's parents bought Brick House for the couple. In 1934, with the Bawdens and Raviliouses both wanting more space to start families, Eric and Tirzah gave up the rent on their London flat and Brick House to move to

EDWARD BAWDEN - DUNKIRK (1940), 1986

Bank House, Castle Hedingham, a few miles east of Great Bardfield. Ravilious used the Essex area profusely in his wood engravings, though many of his watercolours were of Sussex or paintings made during the war. Both he and Bawden became official war artists in the Second World War, and only Bawden returned from the conflict. Ravilious didn't really travel outside of the UK during the war, other than on a boat to Norway, painting instead many of the coastal defences around Britain and some of the airfields, but in 1942 he went to Iceland. While there, he joined a search and rescue team, and their Lockheed Hudson aircraft was lost off the coast. His body was never found. He left behind Tirzah and their three children: John, James and Anne.

Though Bawden survived the Second World War, his time during the conflict wasn't easy either. He joined the War Artists Advisory Committee and early in the war was sent out to paint troops in Northern France, where he found himself on the beach at Dunkirk with the rest of the British Army waiting to be evacuated. He painted and drew while waiting for rescue, which maybe gave him something to occupy his mind in that desperate situation. His quick and accurate sketches have a journalistic accuracy in the draughtsmanship. Later Bawden was shipwrecked off the coast of Africa and was rescued and imprisoned by Vichy French forces. Liberated by the Americans, he was sent off to paint the campaigns in Africa and Iraq. Here he did some of his best work, as his unit wasn't constantly on the move and he could focus on the work. Bawden produced a lot of landscapes and also took up painting portraits of the locals in the Middle East. These skills he would later use for *Life in an English Village* when depicting the villagers of Great Bardfield.

After the war, Penguin Books published

the monograph *Edward Bawden* (1946) in its Penguin Modern Painters series, which included a biographical essay by J.M. Richards, who in 1938 had written the text for *High Street*, illustrated by Ravilious. Richards was married to their friend Peggy Angus, who Ravilious had stayed with at her home, Furlongs, in Sussex before the war.

As the artistic community grew in Great Bardfield, Bawden's work flourished too. He made designs for Wedgwood ceramics, worked for countless publishing houses as an illustrator and painted large murals while having exhibitions of his paintings and linocuts. He was awarded the CBE in 1946 and became a Royal Academician in 1956.

Bawden's style came out of attention to detail and comic wit. Even before his time at the Royal College of Art he was an observant pupil. As a student in the design department of the Royal College of Art, he often mixed calligraphy

and pattern-making in his early works. Though he was a poster designer who was also trained as a painter. Bawden's early watercolours were far from the Victorian style of painting familiar to the public, with a brush loaded with paint on wet paper, bleeding colour across the surface in a misty effect. Bawden's watercolours were drawings layered with crosshatching and short dry strokes of paint. He liked to use papers that allowed him to layer paint and scratch in details. Ravilious's painting style was much the same, though Ravilious also tended to apply paint with a sponge.

As Edward Bawden became older, his paint became thicker, but the line drawings strongly delineating his subject were always apparent. As mentioned earlier, the works Bawden made during the war trained his eye for the drawings in *Life in an English Village*. As a war artist, he got used to sitting in a room and recording all its curious details and inhabitants. Before this, many of his works had been landscapes, not the interior of buildings. Unlike the linocuts he became famous for, the prints in *Life in an English Village*, based as they were on drawings and coloured in tonal bands by the printer, are reminiscent of his watercolours.

EDWARD BAWDEN'S FRONT COVER FOR LIFE IN AN ENGLISH VILLAGE

KING PENGUIN BOOKS

Although published in 1949, *Life in an English Village* in many ways had more to do with the wartime Recording Britain scheme than with the 1951 Festival of Britain. Unlike so many books published after the war, it wasn't looking at a new future; it was recording a world of the there and then. Part of the book's charm is that the village of Great Bardfield appears to be frozen in time. Some might even think that Bawden's illustrations are romantic memories of the past, but the people in the book were real villagers.

At the time, *Life in an English Village* was considered an old-fashioned book, not really a travel book nor an art one. It has been argued it was a reaction to Ravilious and Richards's *High Street*, but Carrington's essay in *Life in an English Village* is broader than Richards's text – which comments on each of Ravilious's illustrations – and covers the way in which village life had been depicted by earlier artists to create the myth of rural, arcadian Englishness. Carrington also writes on the social history of rural life and mentions famous authors who had tackled the subject, but none of it links to Bawden's illustrations directly.

In the late nineteenth and twentieth century, Britain was elegised with the Highways and Byways books. The series started in 1898 with a book on North Wales and was joined by thirty-four other volumes on counties and regions of the British Isles with drawings by contemporary artists. The series set the tone for travel books to come, and in the interwar years of the 1920s and '30s there was a surge in topographical books. Some of these were published by the railways and served as tourist guides for towns and cities on the train lines. Following these guides, and capitalising on the rise in ownership of motorcars after the Second World War, were the Shell guides, which used a lot of photography, and the use of line drawings was consigned to local village guides, normally published by parish councils. Photography played an interesting role in the portrayal of the countryside: while filling it with townies on Sunday drives, it was also putting a focus on conservation. In 1951 Penguin Books started to publish a series of architectural guides of historic buildings in Britain by Nikolaus Pevsner, with each volume normally dedicated to a county.

Penguin published books under various imprints: Pelican (academic topics for a general readership), Penguin (fiction and nonfiction), Puffin (children's books) and King Penguin (monographs). King Penguin books were the publisher's attempt to produce something "more artistic" in hardback to avoid being perceived as merely a paperback company. They were a British

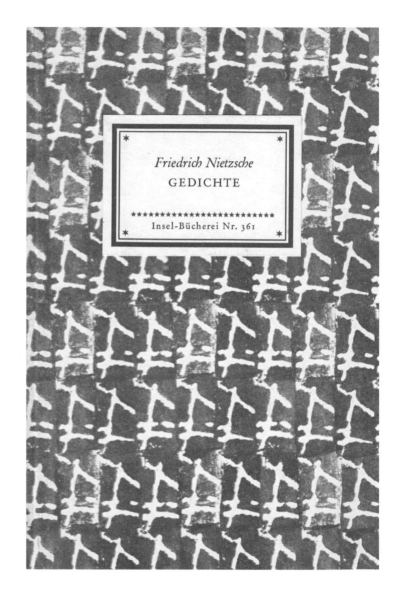

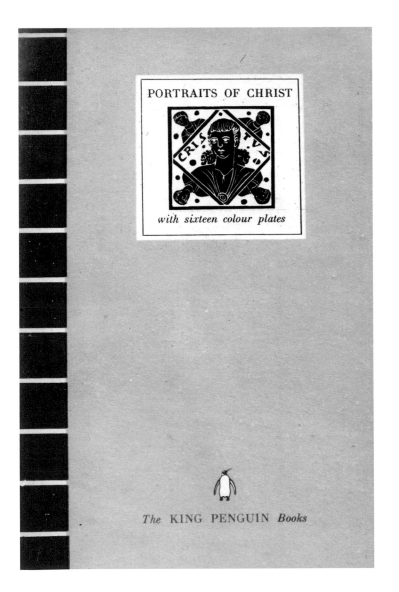

imitation of the Insel-Bücherei series published in Germany by Insel Verlag from 1912 onwards. The size, format and look of the German books, with their patterned covers and colour lithographic plates, were all a direct inspiration. Allen Lane, the head of Penguin Books, wrote that "the aim of the King Penguin is different. These have not been planned to coincide with the public's growing appreciation of art, but rather to appeal to the general liking for illustrated keepsakes of special projects." Mostly these books were for the boffin, the monographs of the connoisseur in the form of a short essay on a topic. Subjects range from lilies and roses to British military uniforms and English ballet.

The first two volumes were *British Birds on Lake, River and Stream* (1939), featuring sixteen plates from John Gould's *The Birds of Great Britain* (1873), with a historical introduction and commentary on each plate by Phyllis Barclay-

Smith, and *A Book of Roses* (1939), sixteen plates from *Redouté's Roses* (1817–24), with a historical introduction and commentary by John Ramsbottom. The third volume had colour plates from a variety of sources rather than reprinted images from an out-of-copyright source.

The editor of the first five books in the series was Elizabeth Senior, a historian and academic who worked at the British Museum as assistant keeper of prints and drawings. Senior also co-wrote the fourth book in the series, *Portraits of Christ* (1940), with her friend Ernst Kitzinger, who had fled Nazi persecution in 1934. Senior was the daughter of Oliver Senior, a teacher at Eastbourne School of Art. She was living with her parents when in 1941 she gave birth to a daughter, Sally Maud, the product of an affair with Sir Thomas Downing Kendrick, who had not wanted her to keep the child. Ten weeks later, Elizabeth died in the Blitz when a bomb exploded on the family house. Sally Maud was found amongst the

wreckage unharmed under a table. Senior's parents and sister, who were sleeping in other rooms in the property, also survived.

The King Penguin series stalled for a while due to the war and Senior's death, but architecture critic Nikolaus Pevsner then took charge as the series editor along with R.B. Fishenden as the technical editor.

There were seventy-six volumes of King Penguin books in total. The scholars providing the texts were famous people at the time, but now most of the books are collected for the work of the illustrators, artists like John Piper, Edward Bawden, Clarke Hutton, Barbara Jones and Enid Marx.

EDWARD BAWDEN - "SUNDAY AFTERNOON", COLOUR PRINTING STAGES

THE PRINTING

"The coloured illustrations in this book are from drawings made by the artist directly on to lithographic zinc plates. They are therefore originals and not reproductions of drawings made on paper."
NOEL CARRINGTON - LIFE IN AN ENGLISH VILLAGE

The quote above from Carrington in *Life in an English Village* has given rise to a misunderstanding that has spread like ripples on a pond. Soon after the volume's publication, Bawden gave fourteen of the drawings for the book to the Great Bardfield historical society, who still own them today.

It was always assumed that to create the lithographs for the book Bawden made the drawings directly on the zinc plates, as Carrington states, but the lithographs perfectly match the drawings. This means the line drawings, done in black ink on paper, were photographed, developed on a glass plate, then transferred onto the zinc, a process used at that time in lithography. The printer then sent the line-drawn proofs for Bawden to colour with watercolour and ink as a guide to the printers. Some of these can be seen on page 118 of *Edward Bawden Scrapbooks* (2016) and feature here. The printers would then negotiate with Bawden on colours, each colour being printed as an individual layer, one at a time. During the printing, the colours would blend together: if blue was printed over a yellow area, it would appear green; green on grey became a light black. With this process, only a few colours were needed to make all the illustrations, so they all have a uniform feeling in tone. For the sixteen colour lithographs in the book, the printers printed eight to one sheet, with the pages registered and the other eight printed on the back to keep costs down. These sheets were then ready to be cut up for binding.

The belief that Bawden drew the illustrations directly onto the zinc plates comes partly from a number of curious mistakes, one being the dog in illustration 13, "The Butcher" (see page 98), with the lines of floor tiles inked behind the hound, and another in illustration 9, "The Cabinet Maker" (page 80), with the ink-drawn outline of a wood frame visible behind a glue pot and through the Primus stove used for warming the glue. In the back, another frame can be seen drawn over a worker's leg. Bawden must have accepted these mistakes, as most readers do. The colour layering makes the objects more whole and by these mistakes take on the feel of a Raoul Dufy painting.

The illustrations were printed by the Curwen Press. Bawden first worked for them in 1925, when he was a student at the Royal College of Art. His tutors Harold Stabler and Paul Nash had introduced him to Oliver Simon, who was a director at the press, which at the time was moving away from its past as a sheet music printer and into printing books and ephemera. Bawden later related, "I went down to the press one day a week as a student, which I thought was thrilling and Harold Curwen, who looked a bit like a scoutmaster, loved explaining how things were done. So I got in among the litho sweats – the men who worked on the litho stones. I did a lot of little tiddley jobs for Curwen. He'd say, 'Oh come down and we'll do a jam label' but he'd spend the time explaining how this or that was done."

At the Curwen Press, Bawden observed how separations were made for each colour area in lithography, and how pen-and-ink was reproduced by line block, and he learnt to adjust his style accordingly. Later he would realise that this was "the last great period of printing, when movable type was used, and interesting".

Malcolm Yorke, in *Edward Bawden and his Circle*, calls the colour of the prints "rather unattractive", but I think their earthy tone is appealing and the use of almost pure cyan is very good. In the days before electric light, and with a shortage of paint after the war, some of these locations must have looked and felt more gloomy than they appear in the book.

AN EXAMPLE OF HOW THE COLOUR LAYERS WOULD SEPARATE

THE ILLUSTRATIONS

THE VICAR

The first colour lithograph featured in the book is of the village vicar, Reverend Kenneth Edward Cartwright. Educated at Keble College, Oxford, he had been a curate in Burnham with Boveney, in Ottershaw and in Choham before settling as curate in Great Bardfield, where he then became vicar from 1921. Bawden illustrates him writing at a desk in a well-furnished study. Cartwright was in his seventies at this time and the vicarage was on Braintree Road in Great Bardfield. He must have had a lot of guests, as there are many chairs scattered around the room. The parishioners he saw here would include couples who wished to be married as well as families arranging christenings and funeral services.

ORIGINAL COLOUR DESIGN ON PRINTER'S PROOF

ST MARY THE VIRGIN

The Anglican church in Great Bardfield is dedicated to St Mary and its earliest parts date from the twelfth century. The large building has a whitewashed interior and a timber beam roof. Largely updated in the fourteenth century, it has two side chapels as well as a rather grand and unusual stone rood screen at the end of the aisle; in the Bawden illustration, the screen is just above the cleaner with her mop and bucket.

The church's font is carved with roses and has a large and ornate wooden cover in gothic style. In the print, the stained-glass windows are brightly coloured and the rest of the interior has a muddy tone. Behind where Bawden would have been sitting are two large glass doors installed in 2003 for the bell tower; they are engraved by Richard Bawden in memory of his parents, Edward and Charlotte.

"The church looks down on one of the most attractive little towns in Essex, full of beautiful old houses. The church, mostly of 14th century date, is remarkable for the stone rood-screen of excellent craftsmanship filling the whole of the chancel arch. The influence of the Catholic Revival is strongly maintained. Two chapels have recently been restored with simple stone altars and good furnishings."
COLLINS GUIDE TO ENGLISH PARISH CHURCHES, ED. JOHN BETJEMAN (1958)

FOUNTAIN AND CHURCH, GREAT BARDFIELD.

ABOVE: THE VILLAGE FOUNTAIN WITH THE CHURCH BEYOND. BELOW: ST MARY'S CHURCH

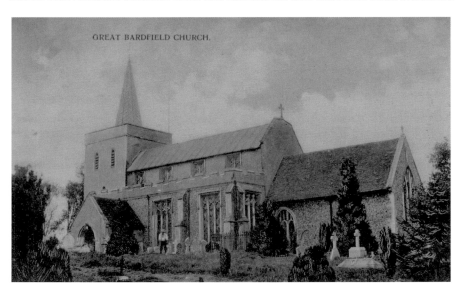

GREAT BARDFIELD CHURCH.

THE METHODIST CHAPEL

The Methodist movement, founded in the 1730s, tended initially to have small groups of followers who held their services in private until congregations and funds grew large enough to build chapels, the first being erected in 1739 in Bristol. The denomination spread over the years, and in the nineteenth century chapels were being built all over the country. Great Bardfield's Methodist chapel, on North Street, was opened in 1862, with seating for 155. The building was sold in 1977 and is now a private residence. Bawden's drawing shows the chapel to be much plainer than St Mary's church, with simpler decorative details.

ORIGINAL COLOUR DESIGN ON PRINTER'S PROOF

THE JUNIOR SCHOOL

The schoolroom has rows of cast iron desks with built-in seating of the kind that forced generations of children to sit and work in a way that was likely their future in the country's drawing offices and banks. The stove to heat the room is behind a small iron guard that wouldn't pass a health and safety inspection today. The headmistress was Miss Irene Duffield, whose domain had clearly not yet become the fluffy world of Joyce Grenfell and her classroom. Miss Duffield had taken up the teaching post in 1926, when she moved from Worthing, Sussex, to Great Bardfield. She was frequently in the newspaper for running events at the school, such as charity fundraisers for the National Institute for the Blind. Her sister was a schoolteacher as well, at White Colne, also in Essex, and her father was once the mayor of Worthing. The photograph below of pupils at the Great Bardfield junior school is circa 1920.

ORIGINAL COLOUR DESIGN ON PRINTER'S PROOF

THE CHILD WELFARE CLINIC

The health clinic might look an antiquated affair, but in 1949 the National Health Service was a new thing, and Bawden, as a socialist, would have thought it worth documenting this revolution in healthcare. The clinic would also have been populated with young children from the post-war baby boom. Before the NHS, children would be bought together to play when one became ill with measles or chicken pox, to encourage group immunity and stop recurrences of the ailment in the village for that generation. The clinic was held in the town hall in Great Bardfield. Built by Henry Smith, the town hall originally housed a horse-drawn fire engine at one side, as seen in the postcard opposite.

ABOVE: THE TOWN HALL, GREAT BARDFIELD. BELOW: BAWDEN'S INK COLOURING OF THE LINE DRAWING

PEELING POTATOES

In one of the most appealing images in the book, the charlady Mrs Buttle is peeling potatoes while cats sit about in the background and laundry dries on racks above. One beautifully executed part of the picture is the curtain over the window. Charladies are now consigned to history and Agatha Christie novels, women who came in to sweep out the fireplaces and prepare them with paper and kindling for lighting later in the day. They would also do other odd jobs, such as preparing food and sorting laundry. Mrs Buttle lived in a cottage on the edge of the village towards Dunmow. One winter, while Bawden was drawing the Friends Meeting House on the High Street, Mrs Buttle threw a snowball at him.

Bawden, who lived on a mostly vegetarian diet, had illustrated cookery books in the past, among them a series for Ambrose Heath, including *Good Potato Dishes* (1935), and was on familiar ground here depicting Mrs Buttle's domain.

EDWARD BAWDEN · FRONTISPIECE FOR GOOD POTATO DISHES, BY AMBROSE HEATH

SUNDAY EVENING

This interior can be identified as the sitting room at Bell Cottage, Bell Lane, the farmhouse for Ives Farm. Farmer Tom Ives is seated with his wife, Lilian (née Hitchcock), who is reading a newspaper, and sister-in-law Maudie Hitchcock, who is reading a book in the foreground.

Around the same time Bawden was working on *Life in an English Village*, John Aldridge, another artist resident in the village, also used Bell Cottage in a series of illustrations for the book *Adam Was a Ploughman* (1947), by Clarence Henry Warren. Viewed together, the illustrations show some items have moved around the room, but there was a two-year gap between the projects. Aldridge's illustration contains the same balloon-back chair that Bawden shows Mr Ives sitting in, and the stuffed animal head on the post can be seen in both illustrations. Below the animal head in Aldridge's drawing is a Currier & Ives print of a boxer, which in Bawden's view is on the wall

to the left below a pair of antlers. In Aldridge's rendition of the Bell Cottage sitting room, the corn dolly that appears in one of Bawden's monochrome drawings for *Life in an English Village* (see page 121) can be seen hanging from a beam in the ceiling. Bawden made a linocut of Bell Cottage in *The Road to Thaxted* (1956), seen below and larger on page 8.

"Tom Ives still had horses on his farm; we had a gate at the end of our garden into the farmyard, where both Edward and several of the other artists used to go and draw, as I did myself."

RICHARD BAWDEN

JOHN ALDRIDGE - ILLUSTRATION FOR ADAM WAS A PLOUGHMAN, 1947

AN AGRICULTURAL MACHINERY REPAIR SHOP

This shows men fixing what looks to be a thresher, tinted in dark blues and browns. There is a large drill press to the left. That the men are busy repairing a horse-drawn machine shows the total automation of the country-side hadn't yet happened in Great Bardfield.

Bawden's drawings in the workshop reveal his quick working, recording in pen and ink what the men are doing. The man in the foreground seems to have many legs, as he has moved while being drawn. It is unknown if Bawden was trying to convey a sense of movement or aiming to perfect the drawing, but the drawing has a photographic quality, as the men are continuing with their work and not posing for the artist. In Bawden and Ravilious's earlier days in the village, these men might also have occasionally repaired carriages like the one pictured in Ravilious's wood engraving *Miss Creed of Little Bardfield* (1934). Miss Creed lived at a house called Chequers on the Thaxted Road with her three sisters and parents. The Creed girls were noted for helping at the child welfare clinic previously pictured.

ERIC RAVILIOUS - MISS CREED OF LITTLE BARDFIELD, 1934

THE CABINET MAKER

The cabinet maker in Great Bardfield was Mr Ernest Alfred Davey, of Cottesbrook, Brook Street. His workshop, attached to the house, is thought to have originally been a coach house of Brook House, once the neighbouring property. Mr Davey, who died in 1951, also worked as a carpenter for a builder as well as making coffins for an undertaker. The site of the workshop building now appears to be occupied by a garage. As cabinets needed precision joining, it is not surprising to see Mr Davey also made picture frames (and, one would guess, stretchers for canvases to be attached to) for the artists in the village. The clutter of activity in the workshop is set against the order of saws and other tools on hooks on the walls and the shelving near the window likely housing boxes of screws and nails. This plate looks to have a few 'errors' in the drawing as well, with lines showing through the leg of the man on the right and the picture frame making a Primus stove and glue pot appear transparent. Was this Bawden throwing aside his perfection in order to show the animation of working? We know he didn't use whiteout paint to remove the lines on the printer's proof line drawings when he added the colour layers, so he must have wanted them to remain.

TWO OF THE TRANSPARENT ELEMENTS OF BAWDEN'S DRAWING

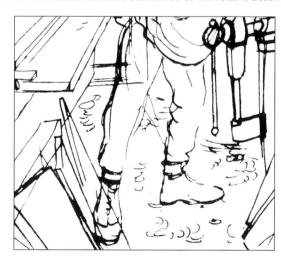

THE BELL

Another good place to see village life is the local pub. In Great Bardfield, that was the Bell Inn. In this lithograph we can see the pints are being pulled by the landlord, Mr Jarrold. The man to the left, smoking his pipe at the bar, is the artist John Aldridge. The policeman in the background is Sergeant Baker, whose police station was next door to Brick House.

The one-eyed man to the right is Fred Mizen, a local man who two years later found himself exhibiting with famous artists at the Festival of Britain. Mizen was born in 1893 at Great Sampford and worked as a farm hand and thatcher for the various farms and houses around the area of Great Bardfield, where he lived and died. Country crafts, like stories, are passed on from person to person, and when seeing corn dollies made in the fields, Mizen took up the craft as a pastime. He served his country in the First World War and in 1917, after losing his left eye and a

finger from his left hand from a gunshot wound, he was honourably discharged. On his return from the war, Mizen worked as a gardener for people in the village and surrounding area as well as doing farm work. He continued making and selling his corn dollies during this time.

During the Second World War, the craft expert and author Muriel Rose came to stay in Great Bardfield with John and Lucie Aldridge while working for the British Council researching and collecting rural craftworks. Rose had owned the Little Gallery, a shop in Belgravia at 5 Ellis Street specialising in artist-designed and craft-made items, but had closed it due to the war. She was introduced to Mizen, likely by John Aldridge and Edward Bawden. Later, in 1946, Rose was working with Bernard Leach to mount a series of exhibitions in the United States, Canada and New Zealand of British rural crafts, and Mizen's works were included in some of these.

In 1951 Mizen (like Bawden) exhibited at the Festival of Britain, for which he had been commissioned to make a giant lion-and-unicorn corn dolly. The figures were seven feet tall and took six months to build. When they were finished they were lightly varnished to protect them from damage. The commission had come in 1950, and part of the publicity machine for the festival was a Pathé newsreel showing Mizen at work. Fred Mizen's figures were a curiosity at the national exhibition. It was an age where art and sculpture were being promoted to the British people as inspiring public works, but Mizen's work was not included on the official sculpture lists for the festival, as they were also considered crafts. After the Festival of Britain ended, the corn dolly was bought by Selfridges and put on display in their Oxford Street department store. Afterwards it was moved to the basement, where, over the next few years, the lion and unicorn figures were destroyed by mice. Bawden featured a collection of Mizen's corn dollies as one of six line drawings in the King Penguin book.

In this illustration of the pub, above the bar on a beam is the last-orders bell and near it a corn-dolly bell that is featured in the monochrome illustration too. On the following pages are two corn-dolly illustrations by Bawden made in 1949, one a line drawing from *Life in an English Village* and the other an engraving made for the Orient Line shipping company.

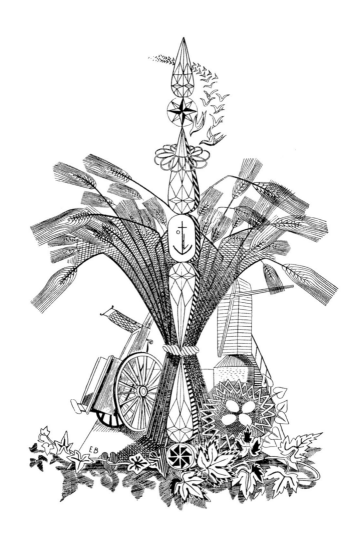

COPPER ENGRAVING FOR THE ORIENT LINE, WITH THE FINCHINGFIELD WINDMILL

LINE DRAWING FROM LIFE IN AN ENGLISH VILLAGE

A VILLAGE STORE

In the days when a village had a butcher, baker and on certain days a market on the site of the old buttercross, the village store would stock vegetables and dry goods such as tea and legumes or other, more luxurious, goods such as sweets and butter. Other than food, it would have sold hardware, as you can see from the lengths of rope and tin baths pictured here. In Bawden's day the shop was Piper's, on Bridge Street. The lady serving at the counter is Betty Clapson and is said to have been serving Mrs Buckland.

On the opposite page (above) is one of the ink and watercolour proofs by Bawden over the printed line drawing. Below is another line drawing Bawden designed for a Labour Party booklet, *Food for Thought*, in 1947, showing the same shop but with the shopkeeper brandishing a knife. On closer inspection he appears to be cutting ham for weighing out for a customer. Edward and Charlotte Bawden were Labour voters and for a time in the late 1940s Brick House was the Labour Party headquarters in the area. The Bawdens were rather progressive and had taken in Republican exiles from the Spanish Civil War as well as two Jewish refugees. The Raviliouses also sheltered a twenty-five-year-old Jewish refugee called Wolfgang Meunzer.

RAVILIOUS ALSO DEPICTED SHOPS, INCLUDING IN THIS WOOD ENGRAVING, DESIGNED AS A BOOKPLATE.

ABOVE: BAWDEN'S INK COLOURING OF THE LINE DRAWING. BELOW: ILLUSTRATION FOR FOOD FOR THOUGHT

THE BAKER

This illustration was inspired by the village's main bakery, opposite Brick House. The bakery in a village would have cooked not only bread but also pies, pasties and cakes, as well as cuts of meat for the villagers. When drawn in 1949, the bakery was in two parts: a kitchen work-shop and the shop, with living accommodation upstairs. In Bawden's illustration, the bread has come fresh out of the oven and is cooling beside the window while more is being freed from the tins by the two women. The baker is using one of the many paddles to reach inside the oven. When the building was later sold, it was converted into a house by the painters Stanley Clifford-Smith and Joan Glass. The couple had lived around the corner in Bucks House, but with a growing family they bought the bakery and enjoyed its large garden and converted the old bake house into Clifford-Smith's studio.

THE BUTCHER

In the drawing for the butcher's shop there is a beautiful set of Lion brand scales and weights ready to measure cuts of meat from the carcasses hung around the shop. The shop was owned by Mr Bone, but locals say he isn't pictured here, and that the staff in the illustration are George Cornell (operating the mincer) and Alfred Smith (serving a customer, named by Malcolm Yorke as Daisy Letch, though others say it is Frances Parker). With so many images in public collections now viewable online, we can confirm that Edward Bawden wasn't the only artist in Great Bardfield to document the people in the village. The painter George Chapman, who moved to the village in 1951, painted the aptly named Mr Bone, though some members of the Bone family dispute that it is him. Who would be a historian?

The butcher's shop in 1949 was located on Vine Street between Barclays Bank and the Vine pub. The bank is now a private house.

Bawden, though mostly vegetarian, made many lithographs with meat and the meat trade as subjects, from cookery books and the lithograph *Cattle Market, Braintree*, published in 1937 by Contemporary Lithographs, to his 1967 linocut *Smithfield Market*, with the carcasses hanging on hooks. In 1946 he also published a lithograph titled *The Produce Shop* in the quarterly *Alphabet and Image*, No. 2 (see page 131). This was always assumed to have been an imagined view, but we now know it was a shop in Great Bardfield that Bawden drew from a postcard, something he rarely did.

TWO VIEWS OF VINE STREET, GREAT BARDFIELD, WITH MR BONE'S SHOP NEXT TO THE PUB

EDWARD BAWDEN – CATTLE MARKET, BRAINTREE, 1937

EDWARD BAWDEN - SMITHFIELD MARKET, 1967

THE TAILOR

Sitting cross-legged in his window to make the most of the light is Mr Fred Suckling, the tailor. This cross-legged position is a traditional posture for tailors at work. Fred was born in Box Cottage, over the road from Bawden's Brick House. Looking like a spiritual leader, he is busy sewing garments and surrounded by the tools of his trade. The iron is likely heated with charcoal or wood shavings that are lit and then placed within rather than a traditional stove-heated iron, which would cool too quickly for linen. To his right, in the foreground, are a sewing machine and a pair of scissors.

For many years he had been a postman in the village, walking up to ten miles a day before he was able to acquire a bicycle. Fred's father was also a tailor, and when he died, Fred took over the family business, returning to the home where he was born. The workshop was located at the back of the cottage.

In this newspaper photograph (left) from his eightieth birthday, Mr Suckling and his wife, Emily (née Hitching) can be seen discussing his work in the same room depicted by Bawden.

THE SADDLER'S SHOP

The leather worker pictured here is Mr Walter Goldstone, of Crown Street. He appears to be not only a maker and repairer of horse saddles and harnesses but also a cobbler of leather shoes. It is suspected that Mr Goldstone is cobbling shoes because, with the rise of mechanical farm machinery, the leatherwork for horses is in less demand.

On the workbench his tools of the trade are spread around, but the clock on the wall is the most impressive item. It was made by the Baird clock company of Plattsburg, New York, to advertise Vanner & Prest's "Molliscorium" emollient for conditioning leather. On this page, in a 1950 press photograph, Mr Goldstone is pictured working at his bench. Opposite is an original receipt from 1923.

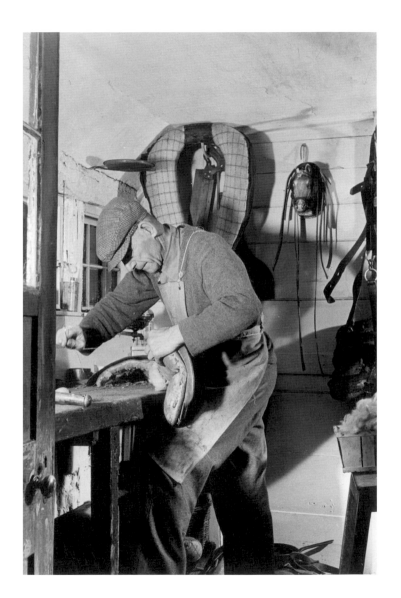

Mich.¹ / 1923

A. W. Ruggles Brise Esq.ʳ Spains Hall & Daivesley Farms acc.ᵗ

Dr. to WALTER GOLDSTONE,
Collar and Harness Maker.

Horses Carefully Measured
and Neatly Fitted.

All kinds of Repairs done
on the shortest Notice
at Moderate charges.

Best and Common Cart Grease
supplied in any Quantity.

Brushes, Combs, Sponges,
Leathers, Compo, Jet Oil, &c.

All Stable requisites kept in stock,
or supplied at shortest notice.

			£	s	d
Aug 1	reprᵍ & patching dett canvas aprons for Binder Machine 3 new Eyletts 5 new thongs 3 new head & 3 new ribs & rivetting & fixing to ditto		1	9	6
2	½ doz helvetia thongs for Binder canvasses			1	6
3	reprᵍ & lengthᵍ chap rein			1	0
13	reprᵍ bitt halter 1 new buckle head & loop to cheek, piecing noseband & new buckle head & loop to rein			4	0
	reprᵍ & lengthᵍ ploughback 1 new head & 1 new swyvel head & swyvel & 1 new dee			3	0
	reprᵍ chap rein 8 one new buckle chap rein 3·6			4	2
Sep 11	reprᵍ & lengthᵍ 2 chap reins			1	9
14	reprᵍ new lining stuffing & restrawing cart collar piecing rim new facing & 1 new side flap to ditto			10	6
		£	2	15	5

THE MARKET GARDENER

In this final lithograph, set inside a greenhouse, colour is thrown about to wonderful effect, layering the chrysanthemums against yellow, then a pool of blue and a darker foreground. The gardener, George Piper, was a member of the family whose shop appears in the lithograph "A Village Store", once located at 11 Bridge Street (then North Street). George Piper and his siblings were living at 5 and 6 Bridge Street in Great Bardfield, in a row of cottages called Rutland Place, built by a local farmer in 1862. The greenhouses stood across the road on the site off Bridge Street where The Willows now can be found. Piper is best remembered for his tomatoes, chrysanthemums and rhubarb.

In Great Bardfield, flower and vegetable cultivation was not only a commercial practice but also a sport. The local horticultural society would have competitions in settings not unlike Bawden's lithograph opposite of a fete from 1946.

THE LINE DRAWINGS

The other illustrations in *Life in an English Village* are six line drawings. These pen-and-ink drawings are groups of similar-themed objects clustered together. The teapots, in a dreamlike landscape of tablecloth and clouds, look like something from *Alice through the Looking-Glass*. The wire plant stands have the look of a Victorian trade catalogue. Many of the Great Bardfield artists collected antiques found in shops, markets and jumble sales, and there is a very good essay on the topic in *The Saturday Book*, No. 5 (1945), by Edwin Smith called "Household Gods". In the post-war era they were all becoming unfashionable.

On page 101 of the monograph *Edward Bawden* (1950), by Robert Harling, is an image supposedly from *Life in an English Village* but which mysteriously isn't found in the book. Could this be a rejected illustration? Given the close relationship between Harling and Bawden and the release of Harling's monograph within a year of the King Penguin book, it is likely that the drawing was indeed intended for Bawden's book and rejected. I've included it on this page.

THE MISSING ILLUSTRATION

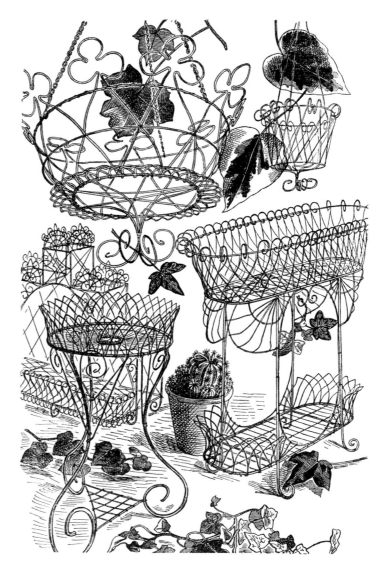

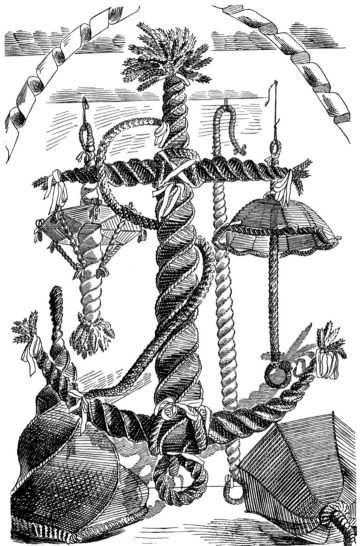

TIRZAH GARWOOD - BRICK HOUSE KITCHEN, 1932

THE ARTISTS' LIVES

When Ravilious and Bawden lodged at Brick House, beginning in 1925, the conditions were primitive but quite ordinary for the time. They had to pump water from a well and had no electricity; their light was from oil lamps, and they used an outdoor lavatory in the form of a bench with buckets underneath that had to be emptied. The property is an early eighteenth-century red brick house with two floors and windowed attics. This Georgian property had been the home of a carriage maker, a girls' school and a coffin maker in its past. The landlady, Mrs Kinnear, had retired as a ship stewardess to manage a butcher's shop in Romford before renting Brick House from Mr Crossman, a local builder. Mrs Kinnear lived in part of the house with one of her daughters, Masie, and Masie's boyfriend, Fred, and their two dogs. The property had two staircases, allowing for the house to be split. Bawden and

Ravilious took four rooms for 7s 6d a week. These came with a shared kitchen and scullery, though the young artists tended to cook on a Primus stove rather than use the kitchen range with the landlady's hen perched on a nest on the side.

As a gift from Tirzah's uncle, Tirzah and Eric had been given a canoe, which they used to navigate the shallow waters of the River Pant. The life ring and a paddle can be seen in one of Eric Ravilious's interior paintings of Brick House, *The Attic Bedroom* (1933). The same canoe was also pictured tied up in Eric's wood engraving *Hovis Mill* (1935) (see page 126). The canoe allowed the Raviliouses and their friends to investigate the local river farther than the villagers could reach on foot, though their passage was blocked by the watermill on the edge of the village. The Pant's source is around the village of Radwinter, fed from aquifers and water running off fields, and it swells in size as it works its way through Great Sampford and Great Bardfield to Braintree, where it becomes known as the Blackwater, which drains into the Blackwater Estuary. The artists caused a commotion in village life on the banks of the Pant when Edward and Charlotte Bawden were still courting. The painter Percy Horton and his wife, Lydia, were staying at Brick House and Ravilious persuaded the group to go for a swim. The Pant, lined with willows and other trees, twisted around the fields skirting Great Bardfield, and at points it was deep and wide enough to plunge into and bathe. One of these spots was provided some privacy by low, old tree branches. As Tirzah recalled, "We hadn't any bathing suits, and conventions and London were forgotten, we went in nakedly and Percy and Eric and Edward threw soft warm mud at each other." Lydia Horton stood and took photos of the proceedings. Many years later, Edward's son, Richard, recorded the memory of this event in his linocut *A Splash in the Pant* (1992).

Any similar fun in the future was spoilt by the young Piper daughters, who all worked in their parents' shop on Bridge Street. The girls had their own rowing boat but due to the low branches couldn't get far along the river. (They can be seen in their boat on page 126.) One day they borrowed Eric and Tirzah's canoe, which allowed them to travel farther, and armed with a saw they cut down the obstructing branches, opening the river up to their boat and giving a clear view upstream of the artists' bathing spot. After this the occupants of Brick House didn't bathe naked again.

During this time, Charlotte and Edward's relationship blossomed. When Charlotte joined the RCA in 1921, enrolling in the design school, she had learnt how to paint and taken an interest in pottery. After the RCA she went into education, teaching art at Cheltenham Ladies' College. In 1928, in the nearby town of Winchcombe, she met the potter Michael Cardew and became an admirer of his work. The following year she was sufficiently inspired

RICHARD BAWDEN · A SPLASH IN THE PANT, 1992

ABOVE: ERIC RAVILIOUS, HOVIS MILL, 1935. BELOW: THE PIPER GIRLS IN THEIR BOAT

to work at the St Ives pottery of Bernard Leach, becoming his secretary and pupil. She had success at the pottery and exhibited in craft shows until 1931, when a kiln fire destroyed most of her work that season and she left the pottery. It was around this time that she became engaged to Bawden. She moved to London and worked for Muriel Rose at her shop the Little Gallery, then lived with Edward in Great Bardfield after they were married. Bawden's father was able to buy Brick House in 1932 for five hundred pounds as a wedding present for the couple. The Raviliouses' wedding present for Charlotte and Edward was a white gazebo, which stood behind the house and features in a few of the paintings and wood engravings made at that time by Eric.

The Bawdens encouraged the Raviliouses to stay on with them, as the house was so large, and for two years a happy cohabitation continued as the husbands painted together. Many friends used to stay with the artists (and before 1932, guests could rent an additional room from Mrs Kinnear). Bawden was assisted in the garden by artist friends Charles Mahoney and Geoffrey Hamilton Rhoades, first clearing up and burying the Kinnears' refuse, then transforming it by digging and planting "the best of everything interesting or unusual in the seed catalogue", according to Tirzah Ravilious. Bawden had a love of sunflowers and chose to allow weeds to stay if they were beautiful enough. Although these artists would be set to work by the Bawdens, either cooking or gardening, they all had time to draw and paint together too. Geoffrey Rhoades painted a view of the back of Brick House and, in another work, the artists gardening in the snow. Percy Horton, Barnett Freedman and other friends of Charlotte's would stay at Brick House, sealing the village's reputation as an artistic place to live.

In 1933 John Aldridge and his lover, and later wife, Lucie Brown (née Saunders), came to Great Bardfield when they bought a large Tudor property called Place House. It was originally the home of William Bendlowes (1516–1584), one of the sergeants-at-law for Elizabeth I, and to this day is a beautiful building. Local rumours (likely untrue) were that as a princess Elizabeth I was kept in hiding there from Mary, Queen of Scots. According to Norman Scarfe's *Essex: A Shell Guide*, Place House has "Tudor brick windows, brick nogging and carved corner bracket" with "W.B. Mense Aprilis A. Dni. 1564" on it. The oldest part of the house dates to the early fifteenth century and was part of a farm and farmhouse complex, with barns and farm to the left of the house and the garden to the right. This was divided into two properties, Place House and Place Farm. *Country Life* once recorded the details of Place House as "a mixture of brick infilling, exposed 16th century beams and plaster, with a Georgian doorway to the street. To one side stand barns and out-buildings, now undergoing conversion to dwellings, and Chapel Cottage, on the other side, also 16th century."

Place House came with a garden of over two acres. It had become a wilderness by the time John and Lucie moved in, as the house has been empty for several years. Rather like the Bawdens at Brick House, the Aldridges went to work, battling primitive conditions in the house and taming the weeds, as the garden provided as much inspiration to John for his work as it did relaxation and food for the couple. Clarence Henry Warren wrote of Place House, "Behind its pleasant facade it hides one of the loveliest gardens I know. The rooks caw in the trees down by its stream – the village church framed in their boughs – and every season brings new joys to light, from the golden pollen dropping from the old cedar in summer to the snowdrops whitening the ground beneath the hazel wood in spring." There was a vegetable garden, nuttery and fruit orchard, beyond which the garden sloped down into a wilderness that would get flooded by Bardfield Brook. In these areas John planted hogweed and more ornamental plants.

With their mighty wedding gift, the Bawdens could redecorate Brick House and make it their own. Tirzah Ravilious noticed that with the Aldridge restoration and redecoration of Place House, interior design became quite a competition between the artists of Great Bardfield and that Bawden would not let himself be upstaged. Modern British artists were decorating their homes in extraordinary ways, from the meticulous interiors of Charles Rennie Mackintosh to the looser and more "monkey see, monkey do" Bloomsbury Group style home decor at Charleston. As home ownership increased in the 1920s, magazines like *The Studio* were documenting artistic design for interiors and spreading the craze. Bawden had a flair for interior design, and in 1926 the Curwen Press printed the Plaistow wallpapers, a series of lino blocks created by Bawden featuring many of his most loved designs. The paper was sold in sheets rather than rolls, and it is not unusual to see them today framed like posters, as some examples are rarer than Bawden's editioned prints. During their Brick House cohabitation, Charlotte and Tirzah learnt how to marble sheets of paper, using petrol and inks in an old tin bath on the table. These would be cut into diamond and lozenge shapes and used to decorate the hall of Brick House.

In the 1950s the living room of Brick House had a hooked rug by Lucie Aldridge in front of the fireplace, while Charlotte's taste for pottery included Winchcombe and Lucie Rie as well as Bernard Leach.

Bawden and Ravilious are now the most famous twentieth-century artists to have lived in Great Bardfield, but they were not the first. The Dutch painter Willem Leonardus Bruckman (1866–1928) lived at Place House for a short time. The sculptor Herbert Hampton (1862–1929) also lived at Place House, from 1927 until his death in 1929, after which it was presumably left empty until the Aldridges discovered it in 1933. Tirzah Ravilious wrote that she and Eric had considered buying Place House themselves, but Eric wanted something simpler to live in than a Tudor house with a strange floor plan. Place House is far from the only curious historical building in the village. Another is the

THE PRODUCE SHOP, GREAT BARDFIELD

EDWARD BAWDEN - THE PRODUCE SHOP, 1946

local lockup, known as the Cage, a small shed-like building with two cells and a door designed to keep either lost cattle or miscreants contained until they could be dealt with by officials. There is also the water fountain at the bottom of the hill by the river, provided in 1860 by the community of Quakers who had taken up in the village and also funded the town hall.

When in 1934 the Raviliouses moved on to Castle Hedingham, they, the Bawdens and the Aldridges were all new home owners, so it is only natural that all of them went to auctions together. They all delighted in Victorian objects, the Bawdens having chinoiserie papier-mâché trays and flatback Staffordshire wally dogs and other figures, and the Aldridges going in for marquetry tables. Lucie Aldridge bought a pair of Derbyshire lion figures standing in front of trees (now in the Victoria and Albert Museum), and both the flatbacks and one of the lions would be depicted by Bawden in one of the monochrome drawings (on this page) in *Life in an English Village*. The artist David Gentleman

LUCIE ALDRIDGE'S PAIR OF SALT-GLAZED STONEWARE LIONS, NOW IN THE V&A

also recalled that the artists of Great Bardfield enjoyed going to "junk-shops, or rather junk-barns full of chests of drawers, iron bedsteads, pictures made of seashells, Staffordshire pots, jardinières made of bent wire, and cast iron fenders and fireplaces".

One thing that did set the Brick House artists apart from the Place House ones was that the Aldridges didn't have children. Lucie was fifty-one by the time she and John, who was sixteen years her junior, got married. The Bawdens had two children: Joanna (b. 1935) and Richard (b. 1936). The Raviliouses had three: John (b. 1935), James (b. 1939) and Anne (b. 1941). Opinion is divided on whether John had wanted children. It was said he was very good with other people's children, but after a pause it would be added that a child was unimaginable in the perfect order of Place House and its garden.

Because Aldridge hadn't been to art school, he learnt the art of printmaking from Lucie (who had been trained by Stanisława de Karłowska) and from Bawden. Together, Aldridge and Bawden

launched another series of wallpapers in 1938, with Cole & Son, called the Bardfield Wallpapers. With the Second World War not far off, it was a bad time to start any business and production had to be paused, but they continued to sell in the 1950s as people had more disposable income. These wallpapers were sold in rolls, making them more desirable to the public. After the war Aldridge and Bawden decorated their homes with them, Bawden having "Periwinkle" in his living room and "Doric" in the dining room.

John and Lucie frequently took the early months of the winter to stay with their friend the writer Robert Graves in the village of Deià, on the island of Mallorca, where John would paint the island landscape. This must have been a relief to Bawden, who at first thought Aldridge would be direct competition as a painter of Essex, but Aldridge also worked mostly in oils and Bawden in watercolours. When the Spanish Civil War came, Robert Graves and his partner Laura Riding stayed in the 'chapel' outbuilding at Place House before going to stay in London and America. Ravilious and Bawden both became war artists in the Second World War and were sent off in various directions to paint. In 1940, John Aldridge finally wed Lucie, in Braintree, to provide her with his pension if he was killed in action. In 1941 the Raviliouses moved from Bank House, Castle Hedingham, to Ironbridge Farm, Shalford, Essex. It was closer to Great Bardfield, and it was to be the last home Eric would know. After being posted all over Britain, in 1942 he arrived at RAF Kaldadarnes, in Iceland. The night before his arrival, another aircraft had failed to return from a patrol, and Ravilious joined the dawn search party to document it. His aircraft was never seen again and he was declared lost in action.

Tirzah stayed on in Shalford until March 1944, when she moved to Boydells Farm, Wethersfield. The following year, Tirzah met the BBC Radio editor Henry Swanzy in Peggy Angus's London house, where Swanzy was a lodger, and in 1946 they married and moved with the children into Ivon Hitchens's old house at 169 Adelaide Road, London. After a number of bouts of cancer, Tirzah went into a nursing home near Colchester, where Christine and John Nash often visited. The home belonged to the sister of Christine's friend Cecil Sharp, and when Tirzah Swanzy died in 1951 she was buried in the graveyard of Copford Church. What of the Ravilious children? Henry's brother John and his new wife Kay took them on. They were send to boarding schools but during the holidays spent time with John and Kay Swanzy in their house in the Cotswolds. James Ravilious became a photographer, whose subject was mostly rural Devon. He married Laurence Whistler's daughter Caroline 'Robin' Whistler. Eric and Tirzah's daughter, Anne, edited her mother's diaries and biography.

During the Second World War the Aldridges would host guests in their 'chapel' building, including the craft and studio pottery expert Muriel Rose and other guests fleeing the Blitz in 1941, such as the artists Michael and Betty 'Duffy' Rothenstein, who had married in 1938. Michael, the son of painter William Rothenstein, had studied at Chelsea Polytechnic and the Central School of Arts and Crafts. Michael was unfit medically to serve in the war, and, liking Great Bardfield, he and Duffy moved into Ethel House, on the High Street. Duffy had been a student at the Central School of Art and was a gifted painter, today most famous for having painted Tirzah Ravilious's portrait in 1944.

With the prospect of being out of work, Michael Rothenstein was picked up by Kenneth Clark's Recording Britain project designed to keep artists in work who were not engaged in the war. Rothenstein painted many views of Essex in 1943 for Recording Britain, including one of Gibraltar Mill, in Great Bardfield. The windmill is of tower design and dates from the early 1700s. There was also a fine watermill in the village on the River Pant that was a focus of travelling artists, but it burnt down in 1993 and only the brick sluice shafts remain. In the early 1940s Rothenstein was a neo-romantic

MICHAEL ROTHENSTEIN · BUTTERFLIES, 1981

KENNETH ROWNTREE · ADAM WITH PRAM, 1943

painter, making modern watercolours of the countryside that had hints of Samuel Palmer, mixing the styles of Bawden's colour pallet and Ravilious's textures.

After the war, Rothenstein concentrated on printmaking, adding a studio onto his house that could contain large printing presses. Like Bawden, he worked in lino but not in the same way; just as Bawden had made linocuts an art form, Rothenstein permanently changed the way British printmaking would be seen with a series of prints and the mixing of medias that were bold and new.

Kenneth and Diana Rowntree were a new addition to the artistic talent in Great Bardfield when in 1941, with the help of Eric and Tirzah Ravilious, they found a house in the village. Kenneth Rowntree was born and raised in Scarborough. His father, the manager of a department store, would display his son's artwork in the shop. Kenneth trained initially to be a cellist then studied at the Ruskin Drawing School, Oxford, and went to the Slade School in London. When war broke out, he joined the War Artists Advisory Committee and worked on the Recording Britain project. Unlike many of the other official war artists, Rowntree was a conscientious objector, leading him to paint not war manoeuvres or military work but rather the peaceful side of the war such as entertainers performing for the troops or foreign servicemen strolling in leafy Hyde Park. Diana Rowntree was an architect who had originally gone to Oxford to read English but switched to architecture at the Ruskin School, where she met Kenneth. She then studied at the Architectural Association School of Architecture. She married Kenneth in 1939 and during the war worked at Jane Drew's architecture offices, designing decoy buildings to fool German bombers, as well as social housing. When Diana found she was pregnant, the Blitz had already started, and wanting a calmer environment to start a family they moved out of the Isokon Building, where they had been living (and as Agatha Christie and

Henry Moore were moving in). In Great Bardfield, they settled into the "handsome draughty" Town House, a few doors down from Brick House. Part of the attraction of Great Bardfield may have been the strong Quaker community. Established in the village in the nineteenth century, the Quakers had their own meeting house off the High Street and were generous in matters relating to the village. The Rowntrees must have found Town House unsuitable, as they moved to the neighbouring village of Lindsell in 1943. They remained part of the Great Bardfield artistic community, however, and Kenneth and Edward Bawden would be involved in similar projects: they both painted murals for the Festival of Britain, and Rowntree, like Bawden, illustrated a King Penguin book, *A Prospect of Wales* (1948), with text by Gwyn Jones.

Bawden had an eventful war. On becoming a war artist he set off, leaving his wife and two children. By his account he was passed between units in the forces like a bad penny, none of them wanting the burden of an artist in their midst. After documenting the dress rehearsal of the Phony War with fellow war artists Barnett Freedman and Edward Ardizzone, Bawden found himself at Dunkirk during the evacuations. Noticing the generals trying to cut in line to leave, he is quoted as saying, "Well, the rats go first." He painted the crisis in the town for two days before boarding a boat and making it back to Britain. Bawden was then sent around Africa, drawing landscapes and local officers, and suffering at times from malaria. Portraiture of this kind was new to Bawden, and he said he had to learn it on the job. It would help him when drawing the illustrations for the King Penguin book. Bawden would later use many of his war drawings to illustrate the collection of poems *Travellers' Verse* (1946), edited by Charlotte's friend Mary Gwyneth Lloyd Thomas.

Bawden, away working as a war artist, had no idea that Ravilious had died on 2 September 1942, and ten days after Ravilious's death Bawden was shipwrecked. He had been travelling back to Britain when his ship, the RMS *Laconia*, was attacked by a German U-boat. The *Laconia* had Italian prisoners-of-war in the hold, many of whom died. Some managed to escape the hold, but on reaching the deck found there were not enough lifeboats. There are various tales of the Italian prisoners being forced to jump into the Atlantic only to be shot in the water to stop them boarding the lifeboats, the blood attracting sharks. Bawden slid safely down a rope and into a lifeboat. An hour and a half after the attack, the *Laconia* sank. Its captain, Rudolph Sharp, having survived when in June 1940 the *Lancastria* was sunk under his command with the loss of three thousand lives, had vowed never to leave a sinking ship again, and so went down with the *Laconia*. Bawden spent three days in the lifeboat before being picked up by the Vichy French ship *Gloire* and driven by truck to a prisoner-of-war camp in Morocco. He developed a lifelong mistrust of the French thereafter, having witnessed abuses and mistreatment of

fellow captives and, earlier, the demoralising jeering by the French directed at the British at Dunkirk. After two and a half months, the camp was liberated by American forces. In the hands of the Americans in Africa, the only way to return to Britain was to cross an Atlantic full of U-boats to New York and then sail back to Britain, running the gauntlet a second time. This did allow Bawden a day of New York City sightseeing.

After his return to Britain at the end of 1942, Bawden was sent to Dunwich, Suffolk, to draw tank and army manoeuvres there, then to draw at Colchester Military Hospital. On his next trip overseas he travelled via Cairo to Baghdad and toured the Middle East, making drawings that would be used to illustrate the Puffin picture book *The Arabs* (1947).

After the war Bawden was in demand as an illustrator, and his war paintings and illustrations were considered successful enough for a monograph on his work to be included in the Penguin Modern Painters series in 1946.

EDWARD BAWDEN - TOWN HALL YARD, GREAT BARDFIELD, 1956

ABOVE: WARTIME GREAT BARDFIELD, WITH SANDBAGS IN FRONT OF THE POLICE STATION. BELOW: ARMISTICE DAY

WALTER HOYLE · GREAT BARDFIELD MILL, 1954

AFTER THE WAR

"Dwindled though Great Bardfield is today, it nevertheless retains a distinct character of its own and, chiefly by the aid of the several artists who have made it their home in recent years, even contributes not inconsiderably to the greater world outside."

CLARENCE HENRY WARREN, ESSEX (1950)

In 1951 George Chapman came to Essex and Great Bardfield with his wife, Kate. His style was expressionist, but he is mostly remembered for his large Welsh landscape works. He studied at Gravesend School of Art and worked in graphic design before deciding in 1937 to become a full-time artist. He studied at the Slade for a year before Barnett Freedman recommended he enrol in the painting school at the Royal College of Art under Gilbert Spencer. Chapman was deaf from childhood and so, like Rothenstein, couldn't serve in the forces during the war, instead teaching at Worcester School of Art. He moved to Norwich in 1945 and married Kate Ablett, a student at Norwich School of Art, in 1947. When they landed in Great Barfield, Bawden cycled over to introduce himself and welcome them to the village. They lived first in Vine Cottage and then moved to Crown House.

Walter Hoyle, who had been working as one of Edward Bawden's assistants for Bawden's Festival of Britain mural (with Sheila Robinson), came to Great Bardfield in 1952. The same year, Stanley Clifford-Smith and Joan Glass came to Great Bardfield, and in 1953 the painter and costume designer Audrey Cruddas moved to Walton House and textile designer Marianne Straub to Trinity Cottage. Finally, in 1954, Bernard and Sheila (née Robinson) Cheese moved to Thaxted, and after their divorce Sheila and her children, Ben and Chloe, moved to Cage Cottage, Great Bardfield. By 1955, Michael Rothenstein had a new studio built for him by Frederick Gibberd, who had just finished the new Heathrow Airport.

With so many artists in one place it was obvious that they should exhibit together. It started with an exhibition in 1942, organised by the Council for the Establishment of Museums and Arts, which included Aldridge, Bawden, Rothenstein, Rowntree and some other locals. But the breakthrough came in 1951 when the community was given a grant by Essex Council to promote an exhibition of paintings as part of the Festival of Britain. This exhibition, rather than being held at a local school or hall, would take place in the artists' own houses, allowing the public to meet the artists, see their creatively decorated homes and then maybe buy a picture to take home. But most importantly, the artists could avoid gallery fees.

Silas Clifford-Smith has done a lot to sum up the mood of the village in the 1950s in his book *Under Moonlight*, a biography of his artist parents, who arrived in Great Bardfield in its heyday. Silas notes: "Being the best known and founding resident artist in the community, Bawden acted like a constitutional monarch, setting the tone of what was artistically acceptable in the village." This is essentially true, but Stanley Clifford-Smith and Joan Glass became a driving force behind the Great Bardfield 'open village' exhibitions.

After the success of the 1951 exhibition, the Great Bardfield artists opened their doors again in July 1954. Bawden, the Aldridges, George Chapman, Rothenstein, Stanley Clifford-Smith, Audrey Cruddas, Joan Glass, Duffy Rothenstein and Marianne Straub all featured in the exhibition. Walter Hoyle met his future wife, Denise Colombo, there. A review of the exhibition in the August 1954 issue of *Art & News Review* said, "The experiment has undeniable attractions. It is pleasant to see work in a non-commercial environment, people buying pictures for the first time." One of the Great Bardfield artists was later quoted as saying they sold far more of their works in these intimate exhibitions than in commercial art galleries in the cities and towns, and in 1958 *The Tatler* would give Bardfield the nickname 'the Montmartre village'.

In July 1955 another exhibition went ahead, with the bonus attraction of David Low, who had taken a cottage in the village. Low, one of the most famous cartoonists in the country, was exhibiting in Stanley Clifford-Smith's house, but unlike the other artists, who would meet and greet browsing visitors, he didn't attend the exhibition, leading to some disappointment in the press.

In November and December 1956 the Great Bardfield artists held an exhibition in the music room at Clare College, Cambridge, a little over thirty miles away. They were joined by other East Anglian artists: Geoffrey Clarke (living in Bury St Edmunds), Denis Wirth-Miller (Wivenhoe), and Eduardo Paolozzi (Landermere). A review in *Granta* magazine concluded that "their styles are as varied as their mediums", with Geoffrey Clarke's and Eduardo Paolozzi's brutal style being in contrast to most of the Great Bardfield artists' work.

From 1957 to 1958 the Great Bardfield artists had a touring exhibition which visited Southend,

Gateshead, Nottingham, Sheffield, Northern Ireland, Eastbourne, Brighton and Wakefield. The exhibition featured the addition of Bernard Cheese and Sheila Robinson. The last open house exhibition was in 1958, when the artists went under the name the Great Bardfield Artists Association. They also hosted Laurence Scarfe and the Canadian artist Peter Whyte.

Michael and Duffy Rothenstein separated after the 1958 exhibition. Duffy went to live in London with the designer Eric Ayres, whom she later married. The artistic community in Great Bardfield had more or less dispersed by the 1960s. Eric Ravilious had died in 1942, Tirzah Garwood in 1951. The Rowntrees moved to Newcastle in 1949 and George Chapman to Wales in 1953. In 1957 Walter and Denise Hoyle moved to the neighbouring village of Great Saling and in 1975 to Bottisham, Cambridgeshire, to be closer to Walter's job at Cambridge School of Art. Michael Rothenstein moved to Stisted, Essex, in 1958. Audrey Cruddas moved to Botesdale, Suffolk, in the 1960s.

Lucie Aldridge separated from John and moved to Cambridge in 1960. Sheila Robinson moved to Saffron Walden in 1968. In 1970 Marianne Straub moved to Cambridge, and after Charlotte Bawden died in 1970, Edward Bawden also moved, to Saffron Walden. Only John Aldridge stayed in the village, living at Place House until his death in 1983.

Unlike the Cornish artists who huddled together and became inspired by each other's works, there was no Great Bardfield school of painting. Many of the artists came to the community with a style that they kept and expanded on, and the only common element in the artists' works was the landscape and farmyards around the village. The legacy of the Great Bardfield artists endures thanks in large part to the Fry Art Gallery in Saffron Walden, which focuses on the work of the artists of northwest Essex.

JOHN ALDRIDGE · GREAT BARDFIELD, 1951

EDWARD BAWDEN - AUTUMN, 1950

NOT FORGOTTEN

"When I got home, I found myself forgotten; another generation of artists had come up. The only people who remembered me was income tax, and their demand was far greater than any money I had in the bank. From then on, I merely resumed the sort of work I was doing before, except the patronage changed."

EDWARD BAWDEN, ANGLIA TELEVISION DOCUMENTARY, 1984

Bawden was prone to sounding pessimistic. His claim that he'd been forgotten after World War Two is quite untrue, but he didn't have a solo exhibition until 1949. His world had changed, and while not forgotten he now worked less as an artist and more as a designer. His time as a war artist was undoubtedly tough, but he proved to be a better artist after the ordeal, having learnt to paint spontaneously in any surroundings, as well as learning portraiture. Nevertheless, after having worked so hard during the war on a constant series of watercolours, the need to produce designs again for other people forced a big adjustment. He had endless amounts of commercial work to get on with: in the two years after the war, he was drawing adverts for zinc manufactures, dust jackets for Albert Camus and Denis Saurat novels, illustrations for *Harper's Bazaar*, designs for Wedgwood ceramics and Ealing Studios film posters and much more. This is partly down to Bawden's ability to work in any field but also to Robert Harling, his champion in the commercial world, who was working for Everetts Advertising and commissioned Bawden as a designer for many jobs, including for Fortnum & Mason.

Proof that Bawden was not forgotten came in 1946, when he was featured in the ninth monograph in the Penguin Modern Painters series. Others in the series' first ten volumes were Henry Moore, John Piper, Duncan Grant and Paul Nash. The slim, mass-printed, affordable book exposed Bawden's work to a wide audience and helped cement his place in the British perception of the art scene. The same year, he was awarded the CBE for his service as a war artist. In 1947 he was elected an associate of the Royal Academy, and in 1956 he became a full academician.

Bawden's 1949 exhibition opened in February at the Leicester Galleries. It contained thirty-eight paintings, mostly made since the end of the war. That summer, Bawden travelled to Canada to teach at the Banff School of Fine Arts. From all accounts, he enjoyed his time teaching there, and he returned to Banff in 1950. His war travels may have inspired him to take on such a distant post, but the chance to paint a new landscape would also have been a welcome challenge. The biggest change in Bawden on his return was his costume; Walter Hoyle commented that he was dressed in blue denim jeans and matching coat, a modern fashion for such a formal chap. After his second trip to Banff, Bawden had enough Canadian watercolours for an exhibition of them in 1951 at the Leicester Galleries. This formed a pattern, and Bawden would have exhibitions after painting trips with artists, such his trip to Ironbridge in 1956 with John Nash and Carel Weight and his trip to Ireland, which yielded two exhibitions in the 1960s.

In 1950 Bawden started to use lino again and designed new wallpapers for Cole & Son. This was swiftly followed with a commission from the Victoria and Albert Museum to produce the print *Autumn*, one of a series of four prints depicting the seasons, the others being done by Gertrude Hermes, John Farleigh and Leon Underwood. Bawden's print (see page 150) featured a gardener tending to tomato plants.

With the commission to make a mural for the 1951 Festival of Britain, Bawden was working on a large scale again for the first time since his mural at Morley College in 1928, which had been destroyed by bombing in the war. The college also commissioned new murals, unveiled in 1958, and in 1966 Bawden made murals for the dining room at BP's London headquarters, which can now be found in the Chelsea and Westminster Hospital.

Bawden never stopped working, but it is for his linocuts that he is best remembered today – for the wallpaper designs he printed with lino in the 1930s, and then for the larger and more confident works in lino, with more colour layers, that he produced in the 1950s. These prints were also lucrative, as they were more affordable than watercolours and could be printed in editions of 35, 50 or 75, or more if there was demand, the prices varying accordingly.

The last big change in Bawden's life came in 1970. With health problems and old age, Edward and Charlotte had been planning to move from Great Bardfield to Saffron Walden, but Charlotte died suddenly on 15 May before it could happen. Bawden's world was thrown into grief, but he honoured the sale and moved to 2 Park Lane, Saffron Walden, alone. That summer, his brightest works, linocuts illustrating Aesop's fables, were shown at the Royal Academy exhibition while, one assumes, his world became slightly darker.

Now Bawden was faced with a fresh problem: the blank canvas of a new house. He set to work decorating the rooms with his own wallpaper designs and possessions brought from Brick House and finally by hanging artwork. The house was transformed into a temple of Bawden.

A studio was built onto the back of the property, with big windows and a trap door for large works to enter the studio without going through the house. By this time Bawden's friend Sheila Robinson was living in Saffron Walden too and he had a new community of friends. The commissions never stopped during these years, and in 1982 Bawden would surprise most people by cutting seventy linocut illustrations for Sir Thomas Malory's *Chronicles of King Arthur* for the Folio Society. With his health failing, his working locations became ever-shorter distances from his home, first views of Audley End, the stately home and parkland a short walk from his house, and then the paintings became not landscapes but interior scenes of his own home. The interiors were mostly populated by his cat, curiously named Emma Nelson, who was called Nelson until he was found to be a she. These works formed the 1987 exhibition "The Private World of Edward Bawden" at the Fine Art Society. Bawden's last two exhibitions, "A Retrospective" at the Victoria and Albert museum and "English As She Is Drawn" at the Fine Art Society, were mounted simultaneously in September 1989. Bawden was due to open the V&A exhibition with a speech, but he had a stroke days before and was recovering in Addenbrooke's Hospital. He died at home in Saffron Walden on 21 November 1989, after working on a linocut of Poseidon.

EDWARD BAWDEN - AND THE SPIES, 1968

EDWARD MORGAN · PORTRAIT OF EDWARD BAWDEN
(THE BENCH, DESIGNED BY BAWDEN, WAS FIRST PRODUCED IN 1956 BY BILSTON FOUNDRIES)

INTERVIEW WITH BAWDEN BY MARTIN GAYFORD

Originally printed in Modern Painters - Autumn 1989. Vol 2. No.3.

I told Edward Bawden why I had come to see him. "Modern painters?" he echoed in surprise. "There are no modern painters in Essex, as far as I know. Anyway, I call myself a designer, not a painter. Out of self-defence mainly. Would you like some tea? Colour all right?" It was – admirably strong.

We were in his drawing-room. The walls were a mosaic of watercolours and prints – by Bawden himself, his son Richard, his mentor, Paul Nash, and his close friend and fellow spirit, Eric Ravilious, who was lost in action while serving as a War Artist in 1942. Outside, in the hall and extending up the stairs, there was an expanse of Bawden wallpaper. On the sideboard, there were a few of the ebullient pieces of china Ravilious designed for Wedgwood in the 30s. All around, in fact, there was ample evidence

of the panache with which Bawden, Ravilious and Nash carried two important traditions of nineteenth century English art into our own day: the vigorous involvement with the applied arts that stemmed from William Morris, and the line of topographical watercolour painting which included Cotman and Turner.

Bawden, himself, in the course of a long life – he is now 86 – has shown extraordinary versatility. He has been a painter, a print-maker, a book-illustrator and a letterer, and designed everything imaginable from textiles to garden furniture. And, in every case, the result has borne his own crisp, humorous stamp.

The day I met him, he was considering the speech he was to give at the opening of the retrospective exhibition of his work at the V and A.

How long would it last? I asked. "How long would you talk for? An hour? Three hours?" I said I thought about two minutes would be my limit. "Exactly", he replied, and grinned conspiratorially.

Tea distributed, I asked about his background. I knew he was born in Braintree, Essex. Did he come from an artistic family? "My parents were ironmongers", he replied firmly. "Of course they weren't interested in art, because they knew very well it would bring in no money, and that was all they thought of. I developed my interest in drawing and painting about the age of six or seven – out of self-defence, I should think. The congregational minister's daughter, who had been to Colchester art school, showed me how to use watercolour – which she did in the Victorian manner, washing yellow ochre over the paper to make it warmer. I never do such things, of course, but she worked in the Victorian fashion."

Had he already discovered, I wondered, the Victorian draughtsmen, such as Edward Lear and

Dicky Doyle, whose boisterous influence is so strong in his work of the 20s and 30s? "No, that wasn't until I went to the Royal College of Art in London. Where could you discover anything in Braintree around 1914? You couldn't discover much – there was the library with a few novels, mainly for women, and copies of the *Boy's Own Paper* and the *Girl's Own Paper*, the latter being much more interesting. Then, when I was at the Friend's School at Saffron Walden, I used to draw in the afternoons while other boys were playing games. I never played games, because I had a strained heart. Later I went to Cambridge, to the School of Art, and I studied lettering, which I did because it was a choice between lettering and illuminating or metal-work, which is a noisy craft. So I picked lettering because I didn't like the banging. I was taught by a young man who had been at the Royal College of Art under Edward Johnston, who made a big name for himself by that book he produced. I can still cut a quill-pen, even now."

Next he went to the Royal College of Art on a design scholarship. Why design? "I had to get a scholarship to get to London. My parents didn't have the money, and anyway, why support a worthless young man – who's never going to make any money himself? There were only twelve scholarships in the whole of the country – twelve for painting, twelve for sculpture, twelve for design. So I chose design because I thought I'd stand more chance. In those days, if I'd chosen sculpture for example, I'd have been likely to be up against someone like Henry Moore, who would certainly have got it. In fact, in my year he did. So I became interested in design, and I became a designer, rather than a painter or a sculptor.

"I started working when I was still a student, after I met Harold Curwen of the Curwen Press. Jobs came along – doing a tiny drawing for the Westminster Bank, or for BP. For a long time I was doing one or two drawings for BP every week, and they paid extremely well – £9 for each drawing. I was rich. They had their copywriters and there I met Betjeman, acting the fool and making some good — what do you call them, captions, and entertaining his boss, who was Beddington, a big noise in advertising in those days. I did hundreds of tiny little drawings for BP not much bigger than that. I put Venice into that amount of space." He held his finger and thumb about an inch and a half apart.

Did he enjoy doing this commercial work? "I enjoyed making money. What would my father have said if I hadn't. He had no opinion whatsoever of my ability as an artist."

Was that when he started doing wallpaper? "Oh, that was done when I was very young. I used linoleum as a surface to print on; I would go out and get a shilling's worth, which was soft in those days, and hacked away with my pen-knife, and printed it with oil-paint. I'd just cut a cow, about so big, and by repeating it I'd get a herd. The pattern arose quite naturally from the little blocks I cut. I didn't have to sit down with a pencil, and painfully work out a repeat; it worked itself out. And Paul Nash, when he was teaching us, suggested an exchange. That's what he gave me." He pointed at four Paul Nash wood-cuts*, framed together and hanging in the corner of the room. What had Bawden given in return? "Bits of wallpaper which I'd printed myself, on the floor in front of the fire in my bed-sit. Later on I sold the idea to Harold Curwen, who reproduced them by lithography, but not many shops took it up. There was one in Bedford Square, which sold most of my produce, but after six years of it sitting there, I think I had only made six pounds. They were sold in sheets. There's a prejudice against selling wallpaper in sheets, which is quite unnecessary."

I said this neglect was a shame, since his are among the best English wallpapers since William Morris. He thought about this. "Well, a good pattern is as good as a painting. I'd sooner have

* THE PRINTS BAWDEN RECEIVED FROM NASH WERE FOUR OF NASH'S ILLUSTRATIONS OF THE NONESUCH PRESS BOOK GENESIS, 1924, AND AN ENGRAVING, THE BAY, 1923.

a good bit of Morris than I would a lot of modern rubbish."

Earlier on, I reminded him, he had said he called himself a designer not a painter. Why was that? "Because it's true. I love design, I love putting things together – it's often very difficult. I like the complexity you're sometimes faced with. I did a book on the Arabs with a drawing of the Arabs and the Persians fighting – the Battle of al-Qadisiyyah – I love doing that sort of thing. I prefer many of the old stories such as one finds in Herodotus or in the Bible to present day stories one finds in a book. I think there's much wider scope in design. When I'm on good form, I get to some point in the design and I laugh and talk, and if I'm laughing, it probably means the work is rather good."

Is humour important to him? "Well, one can't help that, perhaps. At any rate, I think you shouldn't take anything too seriously, otherwise it won't come out right."

I remarked that Bawden had worked in more different areas of painting and design than almost any other artist I could think of. "Perhaps so, I don't want to spend my life doing just one thing. I think there's much more scope in design." Bawden is also one of the finest topographical watercolourists of the century. When had he started?

"When I moved to Great Bardfield in Essex, which I did because I met a writer, A.J.A. Symons, who had made a great success writing a book about Baron Corvo, and he lived in the country at Finchingfield. So one day Douglas (Percy) Bliss and I went down by train and then cycled on to Bardfield. It was wonderful in those days. It was a real village, it had three or four tailors and three or four bakers and so on; the food didn't come from Braintree, it was made on the spot. I started living in Brick House in Bardfield in 1932 [in fact it was 1925], we rented it for, I think, ten shillings a week. Eric Ravilious and his family lived in the other half of the house. Eric and I both wanted to paint the countryside. Of course, farming was lovely then. You'd see great machines going round cutting the corn. John Nash has made

drawings of all that. It looked lovely. Nowadays, of course, fields are thrown into other fields to make great big open spaces, which is horrible. Destroys hedgerows, destroys birds and other animals. There's hardly an animal the size of a mouse to be found in the country now. I love wild creatures."

I added that there were now more foxes in the suburbs than in the open country. "Yes, I wouldn't mind hunting the hunting people. With bows and arrows, I should think, so the arrows can stick in tender parts." He paused thoughtfully. "You go hunting, do you?" I said I didn't.

Changing the subject, I asked if Bawden had any example in mind when he started painting landscapes? "We knew the earlier painters, of course, Turner and all the rest of them. There were masses and masses of them, all very good. But different generations work in different ways. I never use watercolour in a sloppy sort of way, but rather tightly. The generation before ours slopped the colour on, I use it rather dry, and on a non-absorbent paper, a very hard Whatman –

pure white, which gives brilliancy – which was then used for writing and illuminating. You could draw on it with a quill beautifully, but the colour stayed rather on the surface so it was possible to wash out quite easily. Ravilious and I were often in the bathroom at the end of a day's work, washing out what we had done." "Under the tap?" I suggested. "In the bath."

The watercolours Bawden painted during the Second World War, in which he served as an official War Artist were looser and more confident in handling. Why was that? "Well, things were rather different. One had to hurry. One might be in a street, and the cry would go up, 'The Germans are coming!' and one got behind a door."

Did he find his work as a war artist inspiring? "Do you find the north of France inspiring?" I replied that I didn't. "Not a bit, no, I enjoyed working in Africa, though, because there were wild beasts around, also because I walked from the Sudan into Abyssinia, which took

several weeks. I like adventure. I painted Haile Selassie's palace, which wasn't much – rather like the building at Kew. I didn't find Abyssinia a romantic place, I found it a place to have about five weeks in hospital with malaria. But I like black chaps, and there were lots of them at Omdurman at the training depot. One had to be so spry, though, often a very picturesque man might walk into camp and talk to someone, but the conversation wouldn't go on long enough, possibly, to get the drawing done. One had to be so fast. But if you caught them at the right time, during Ramadan, when they are not eating and drinking during the day, you could draw them as easy as flowers."

Bawden, who is a terrifically hard worker, continued to paint and draw despite being shipwrecked and interned in a POW camp. I asked him about the experience. "Yes, we were torpedoed. I don't advise you to let that happen. The sharks may be interested, they were generally nosing all around the raft." "How long was it before you were rescued?" "Not long, about five or six days, I think, before the Vichy French picked us up. We cheered, thinking they were on our side, but they weren't. I had a little paper, so I did a few drawings. But paper was too valuable, really, it went to the behind."

At this point, we wandered next door, to watch Bawden's grandson, Philip, producing a large colour-print of a leaping frog, which was to be sold in conjunction with the exhibition at the V and A. Bawden lamented the paucity of frogs in East Anglia these days. "They have special road-crossings for them in Cornwall, you know." I reassured him that my own garden in Cambridge was jumping with little green bodies, and the conversation turned entirely to amphibians.

THOMAS HENNELL - EGDON HEATH, INK DRAWING, 1938/9
ORIGINAL ARTWORK FOR A COUNTRYMAN'S JOURNAL, BY H.J. MASSINGHAM, 1939

BIBLIOGRAPHY

HELEN BINYON
ERIC RAVILIOUS: MEMOIR OF AN ARTIST
2016, LUTTERWORTH PRESS

SILAS CLIFFORD-SMITH
UNDER MOON-LIGHT
2015, SILAS CLIFFORD-SMITH

OLIVE COOK AND ANDREW LAMBIRTH
ARTISTS AT THE FRY
2012, THE FRY ART GALLERY

ANDY FRIEND
RAVILIOUS & CO: THE PATTERN OF FRIENDSHIP
2017, THAMES & HUDSON

TIRZAH GARWOOD
LONG LIVE GREAT BARDFIELD
2016, PERSEPHONE BOOKS

NORMAN SCARFE
ESSEX: A SHELL GUIDE
1968, FABER & FABER

W.J. STRACHAN
"THE ARTISTS OF GREAT BARDFIELD"
THE STUDIO, MARCH 1958
VOL. 155 NO. 780

JEAN VACHER
MURIEL ROSE: A MODERN CRAFTS LEGACY
2006

C. HENRY WARREN
ESSEX
1950, ROBERT HALE

C. HENRY WARREN
"HEART OF ESSEX"
THE COUNTRYGOER
1948, VOL LIV

C. HENRY WARREN
"THOMAS HENNELL"
THE COUNRYMAN
1957, AUTUMN, VOL LIV, NO.3

MALCOLM YORKE
EDWARD BAWDEN AND HIS CIRCLE
2007, ANTIQUE COLLECTORS' CLUB

GILL SAUNDERS & MALCOLM YORKE, EDS.
BAWDEN, RAVILIOUS AND THE ARTISTS OF GREAT BARDFIELD
2015, V&A

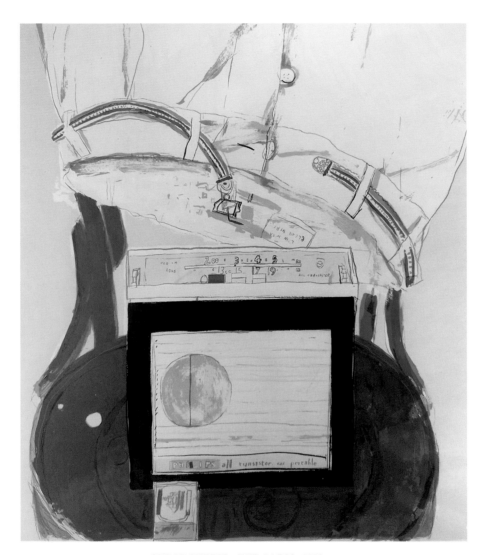

CHLOE CHEESE - THE RADIO, 1982

IMAGE REFERENCES

FRONT COVER – EDWARD BAWDEN – "THE MARKET GARDENER", FROM *LIFE IN AN ENGLISH VILLAGE*, 1949, KING PENGUIN BOOKS, © ESTATE OF EDWARD BAWDEN. SOURCE – INEXPENSIVE PROGRESS.

PAGE 2 – EDWARD BAWDEN – COVER DEVICES, EDITED, FROM *LIFE IN AN ENGLISH VILLAGE*, 1949, KING PENGUIN BOOKS, © ESTATE OF EDWARD BAWDEN. SOURCE – INEXPENSIVE PROGRESS.

PAGE 3 – EDWARD BAWDEN – *THE LION AND THE UNICORN*, © ESTATE OF EDWARD BAWDEN. SOURCE – FRY ART GALLERY.

PAGE 5 – EDWARD BAWDEN – DETAIL OF PRINTER'S PROOF OF "THE VICAR", FOR *LIFE IN AN ENGLISH VILLAGE*, KING PENGUIN BOOKS, © ESTATE OF EDWARD BAWDEN. SOURCE – INEXPENSIVE PROGRESS.

PAGE 6 – CHLOE CHEESE – *GREAT BARDFIELD CAT*, 2010, © CHLOE CHEESE. SOURCE – FRY ART GALLERY.

PAGE 8 – EDWARD BAWDEN – *THE ROAD TO THAXTED*, 1956, © ESTATE OF EDWARD BAWDEN. SOURCE – FRY ART GALLERY.

PAGE 11 – (TOP) T.A. LETCH STORES. SOURCE – STELLA HERBERT; (BOTTOM) THE CARNIVAL IN GREAT BARDFIELD. SOURCE – STELLA HERBERT.

PAGE 12 – (TOP) SHEILA ROBINSON – *BROOK STREET, GREAT BARDFIELD*, 1991, © ESTATE OF SHEILA ROBINSON. SOURCE – FRY ART GALLERY; (BOTTOM) BROOK STREET, GREAT BARDFIELD. SOURCE – STELLA HERBERT.

PAGE 14 – (TOP) HARVESTING FIELDS, GREAT BARDFIELD. SOURCE – STELLA HERBERT; (BOTTOM) CORONATION DECORATIONS, GREAT BARDFIELD. SOURCE – STELLA HERBERT.

PAGE 17 – EDWARD BAWDEN – *GREAT LODGE FARM*, ZINC ADVERT, 1945, © ESTATE OF EDWARD BAWDEN. SOURCE – INEXPENSIVE PROGRESS.

PAGE 18 – THOMAS HENNELL – *FLAIL THRESHING*, SEPTEMBER 1944. SOURCE – INEXPENSIVE PROGRESS.

PAGE 19 – EDWARD BAWDEN – FARM DRAWING, 1947, © ESTATE OF EDWARD BAWDEN. SOURCE – INEXPENSIVE PROGRESS.

PAGE 21 – EDWARD BAWDEN – PRINTER'S PROOF FOR *THE ARABS*, PUFFIN BOOKS, © ESTATE OF EDWARD BAWDEN. SOURCE – INEXPENSIVE PROGRESS.

PAGE 22 – DORA CARRINGTON – *NOEL CARRINGTON*, 1918, © ESTATE OF DORA CARRINGTON. SOURCE – THE HIGGINS BEDFORD.

PAGE 25 – ERIC RAVILIOUS – (TOP) "MAY", *THE COUNTRY LIFE COOKERY BOOK*, 1937; (BOTTOM) "OCTOBER", *THE COUNTRY LIFE COOKERY BOOK*, 1937. SOURCE – INEXPENSIVE PROGRESS.

PAGE 26 – ERIC RAVILIOUS – (TOP) DECORATION FROM *THE KYNOCH PRESS NOTE BOOK*, 1932, G.219. SOURCE – INEXPENSIVE PROGRESS; (BOTTOM) *AUTUMN FRUITS*, 1936, G.348. SOURCE – INEXPENSIVE PROGRESS.

PAGE 27 – COLLECTION OF PUFFIN PICTURE BOOKS. SOURCE – INEXPENSIVE PROGRESS.

PAGE 28 – DAVID EVAN EDWARDS – *EDWARD BAWDEN*, 1974. SOURCE – FRY ART GALLERY.

PAGE 30 – ERIC RAVILIOUS – *BRICK HOUSE*, 1933, PRINT. SOURCE – STELLA HERBERT.

PAGE 31 – HIGH STREET, GREAT BARDFIELD, POSTCARD. SOURCE – STELLA HERBERT.

PAGE 32 – EDWARD BAWDEN – *DUNKIRK (1940)*, 1986, © ESTATE OF EDWARD BAWDEN. SOURCE – INEXPENSIVE PROGRESS.

PAGE 34 – EDWARD BAWDEN – LINE DRAWING FROM *LIFE IN AN ENGLISH VILLAGE*, 1949, KING PENGUIN BOOKS, © ESTATE OF EDWARD BAWDEN. SOURCE – INEXPENSIVE PROGRESS.

PAGE 35 – EDWARD BAWDEN – *TRAIN* , DECORATION FROM *THE KYNOCH PRESS NOTE BOOK*, 1936, © ESTATE OF EDWARD BAWDEN. SOURCE – INEXPENSIVE PROGRESS.

PAGE 36 – EDWARD BAWDEN – FRONT COVER OF *LIFE IN AN ENGLISH VILLAGE*, KING PENGUIN BOOKS, 1949, © ESTATE OF EDWARD BAWDEN. SOURCE – INEXPENSIVE PROGRESS.

PAGE 38 – FRIEDRICH NIETZSCHE, *GEDICHTE*, INSEL-BUCHERIE 361, INSEL VERLAG, 1956.

PAGE 39 – ERNST KITZINGER AND ELIZABETH SENIOR, *PORTRAITS OF CHRIST*, KING PENGUIN BOOKS, 1940. SOURCE – INEXPENSIVE PROGRESS.

PAGE 40 – PHYLLIS BARCLAY-SMITH, *WOODLAND BIRDS*, KING PENGUIN BOOKS, 1955. SOURCE – INEXPENSIVE PROGRESS.

PAGE 41 – R.M. LOCKLEY, *BIRDS OF THE SEA*, KING PENGUIN BOOKS, 1945, COVER DESIGN BY ENID MARX. SOURCE – INEXPENSIVE PROGRESS.

PAGE 42 – EDWARD BAWDEN – COLOUR PRINTING STAGES FOR "SUNDAY AFTERNOON", FOR *LIFE IN AN ENGLISH VILLAGE*, 1949, KING PENGUIN BOOKS, © ESTATE OF EDWARD BAWDEN. SOURCE – INEXPENSIVE PROGRESS.

PAGE 45 – EDWARD BAWDEN – PRINTER'S PROOF OF "THE BUTCHER", FOR *LIFE IN AN ENGLISH VILLAGE*, 1949, KING PENGUIN BOOKS, © ESTATE OF EDWARD BAWDEN. SOURCE – INEXPENSIVE PROGRESS.

PAGE 46 – EDWARD BAWDEN – "THE CHILD WELFARE CLINIC", FROM *LIFE IN AN ENGLISH VILLAGE*, 1949, KING PENGUIN BOOKS, IMAGINED COLOUR SEPARATIONS, EDITED, ORIGINAL IMAGE FROM BRIAN WEBB AND PEYTON SKIPWITH, *EDWARD BAWDEN SCRAPBOOKS*, 2016, LUND HUMPHRIES, © ESTATE OF EDWARD BAWDEN. SOURCE – FRY ART GALLERY.

PAGE 48 – EDWARD BAWDEN – COVER DEVICE FROM *LIFE IN AN ENGLISH VILLAGE*, 1949, KING PENGUIN BOOKS, EDITED, © ESTATE OF EDWARD BAWDEN. SOURCE – INEXPENSIVE PROGRESS.

PAGE 49 – EDWARD BAWDEN – "THE VICAR", FROM *LIFE IN AN ENGLISH VILLAGE*, 1949, KING PENGUIN BOOKS, © ESTATE OF EDWARD BAWDEN. SOURCE – FRY ART GALLERY.

PAGE 50 – EDWARD BAWDEN – PRINTER'S PROOF OF "THE VICAR", FOR *LIFE IN AN ENGLISH VILLAGE*, 1949, KING PENGUIN BOOKS, © ESTATE OF EDWARD BAWDEN. SOURCE – INEXPENSIVE PROGRESS.

PAGE 51 – EDWARD BAWDEN – ORIGINAL COLOUR DESIGN FOR "THE VICAR", FOR *LIFE IN AN ENGLISH VILLAGE*, 1949, KING PENGUIN BOOKS, FROM BRIAN WEBB AND PEYTON SKIPWITH, *EDWARD BAWDEN SCRAPBOOKS*, 2016, LUND HUMPHRIES, © ESTATE OF EDWARD BAWDEN. SOURCE – FRY ART GALLERY.

PAGE 53 – EDWARD BAWDEN – "ST MARY THE VIRGIN", FROM *LIFE IN AN ENGLISH VILLAGE*, 1949, KING PENGUIN BOOKS, © ESTATE OF EDWARD BAWDEN. SOURCE – INEXPENSIVE PROGRESS.

PAGE 54 – (LEFT) ERIC RAVILIOUS – DECORATION FROM *THE KYNOCH PRESS NOTE BOOK*, 1933, G.208. SOURCE – INEXPENSIVE PROGRESS; (RIGHT) ERIC RAVILIOUS – *THE VILLAGE*, 1933. SOURCE – INEXPENSIVE PROGRESS.

PAGE 55 – (ABOVE) POSTCARD OF THE VILLAGE FOUNTAIN, GREAT BARDFIELD. SOURCE – STELLA HERBERT; (BELOW) POSTCARD OF THE CHURCH AT GREAT BARDFIELD. SOURCE – STELLA HERBERT.

PAGE 57 – EDWARD BAWDEN – "THE METHODIST CHAPEL", FROM *LIFE IN AN ENGLISH VILLAGE*, 1949, KING PENGUIN BOOKS, © ESTATE OF EDWARD BAWDEN. SOURCE – INEXPENSIVE PROGRESS.

PAGE 58 – EDWARD BAWDEN – PRINTER'S PROOF OF "THE METHODIST CHAPEL", FOR *LIFE IN AN ENGLISH VILLAGE*, 1949, EDITED, © ESTATE OF EDWARD BAWDEN. SOURCE – INEXPENSIVE PROGRESS.

PAGE 59 – EDWARD BAWDEN – ORIGINAL COLOUR DESIGN FOR "THE METHODIST CHAPEL", FOR *LIFE IN AN ENGLISH VILLAGE*, 1949, KING PENGUIN BOOKS, FROM BRIAN WEBB AND PEYTON SKIPWITH, *EDWARD BAWDEN SCRAPBOOKS*, 2016, LUND HUMPHRIES, © ESTATE OF EDWARD BAWDEN. SOURCE – FRY ART GALLERY.

PAGE 61 – EDWARD BAWDEN – "THE JUNIOR SCHOOL", FROM *LIFE IN AN ENGLISH VILLAGE*, 1949, KING PENGUIN BOOKS, © ESTATE OF EDWARD BAWDEN. SOURCE – INEXPENSIVE PROGRESS.

PAGE 62 – POSTCARD OF THE VILLAGE SCHOOL, GREAT BARDFIELD. SOURCE – STELLA HERBERT.

PAGE 63 – EDWARD BAWDEN – ORIGINAL COLOUR DESIGN FOR "THE JUNIOR SCHOOL", FOR *LIFE IN AN ENGLISH VILLAGE*, 1949, KING PENGUIN BOOKS, FROM BRIAN WEBB AND PEYTON SKIPWITH, *EDWARD BAWDEN SCRAPBOOKS*, 2016, LUND HUMPHRIES, © ESTATE OF EDWARD BAWDEN. SOURCE – FRY ART GALLERY.

PAGE 65 – EDWARD BAWDEN – "THE CHILD WELFARE CLINIC", FROM *LIFE IN AN ENGLISH VILLAGE*, 1949, KING PENGUIN BOOKS, © ESTATE OF EDWARD BAWDEN. SOURCE – INEXPENSIVE PROGRESS.

PAGE 66 – EDWARD BAWDEN – (TOP) DETAILS FROM THE GENERAL HOSPITAL, ZINC ADVERT, 1945, © ESTATE OF EDWARD BAWDEN. SOURCE – INEXPENSIVE PROGRESS; (BOTTOM) EDWARD BAWDEN – DETAIL FROM "THE CHILD WELFARE CLINIC", FROM *LIFE IN AN ENGLISH VILLAGE*, 1949, KING PENGUIN BOOKS, © ESTATE OF EDWARD BAWDEN. SOURCE – INEXPENSIVE PROGRESS.

PAGE 67 – (TOP) THE TOWN HALL, GREAT BARDFIELD. SOURCE – STELLA HERBERT; (BOTTOM) EDWARD BAWDEN – ORIGINAL COLOUR DESIGN FOR "THE CHILD WELFARE CLINIC", FOR *LIFE IN AN ENGLISH VILLAGE*, 1949, KING PENGUIN BOOKS, FROM BRIAN WEBB AND PEYTON SKIPWITH, *EDWARD BAWDEN SCRAPBOOKS*, 2016, LUND HUMPHRIES, © ESTATE OF EDWARD BAWDEN. SOURCE – FRY ART GALLERY.

PAGE 69 – EDWARD BAWDEN – "PEELING POTATOES", FROM *LIFE IN AN ENGLISH VILLAGE*, 1949, KING PENGUIN BOOKS, © ESTATE OF EDWARD BAWDEN. SOURCE – INEXPENSIVE PROGRESS.

PAGE 70 – EDWARD BAWDEN – DETAILS FROM PRINTER'S PROOF OF "PEELING POTATOES", FOR *LIFE IN AN ENGLISH VILLAGE*, 1949, KING PENGUIN BOOKS, © ESTATE OF EDWARD BAWDEN. SOURCE – INEXPENSIVE PROGRESS.

PAGE 71 – EDWARD BAWDEN – FRONTISPIECE FROM AMBROSE HEATH, *GOOD POTATO DISHES*, 1935, FABER AND FABER. © ESTATE OF EDWARD BAWDEN. SOURCE – INEXPENSIVE PROGRESS.

PAGE 73 – EDWARD BAWDEN – "SUNDAY EVENING", FROM *LIFE IN AN ENGLISH VILLAGE*, 1949, KING PENGUIN BOOKS, © ESTATE OF EDWARD BAWDEN. SOURCE – INEXPENSIVE PROGRESS.

PAGE 74 – EDWARD BAWDEN – *THE ROAD TO THAXTED*, 1956 , © ESTATE OF EDWARD BAWDEN. SOURCE – FRY ART GALLERY.

PAGE 75 – JOHN ALDRIDGE – ILLUSTRATION FROM CLARENCE HENRY WARREN, *ADAM WAS A PLOUGHMAN*, 1947, EYRE AND SPOTTISWOODS, © ESTATE OF JOHN ALDRIDGE. SOURCE – INEXPENSIVE PROGRESS.

PAGE 77 – EDWARD BAWDEN – "AN AGRICULTURAL MACHINERY REPAIR SHOP", FROM *LIFE IN AN ENGLISH VILLAGE*, 1949, KING PENGUIN BOOKS, © ESTATE OF EDWARD BAWDEN. SOURCE – INEXPENSIVE PROGRESS.

PAGE 78 – EDWARD BAWDEN – DETAILS FROM PRINTER'S PROOF OF "AN AGRICULTURAL MACHINERY REPAIR SHOP", FOR *LIFE IN AN ENGLISH VILLAGE*, 1949, KING PENGUIN BOOKS, © ESTATE OF EDWARD BAWDEN. SOURCE – INEXPENSIVE PROGRESS.

PAGE 79 – ERIC RAVILIOUS – *MISS CREED OF LITTLE BARDFIELD*, 1934. SOURCE – INEXPENSIVE PROGRESS.

PAGE 81 – EDWARD BAWDEN – "THE CABINET MAKER", FROM *LIFE IN AN ENGLISH VILLAGE*, 1949, KING PENGUIN BOOKS, © ESTATE OF EDWARD BAWDEN. SOURCE – INEXPENSIVE PROGRESS.

PAGE 82 – EDWARD BAWDEN – COVER DEVICE, EDITED, FROM *LIFE IN AN ENGLISH VILLAGE*, 1949, KING PENGUIN BOOKS, © ESTATE OF EDWARD BAWDEN. SOURCE – INEXPENSIVE PROGRESS.

PAGE 83 – EDWARD BAWDEN – DETAILS FROM PRINTER'S PROOF OF "THE CABINET MAKER", FOR *LIFE IN AN ENGLISH VILLAGE*, 1949, KING PENGUIN BOOKS, © ESTATE OF EDWARD BAWDEN. SOURCE – INEXPENSIVE PROGRESS.

PAGE 85 – EDWARD BAWDEN – "THE BELL", FROM *LIFE IN AN ENGLISH VILLAGE*, 1949, KING PENGUIN BOOKS, © ESTATE OF EDWARD BAWDEN. SOURCE – INEXPENSIVE PROGRESS.

PAGE 86 – EDWARD BAWDEN – DETAIL FROM PRINTER'S PROOFS OF "THE BELL", FOR *LIFE IN AN ENGLISH VILLAGE*, 1949, KING PENGUIN BOOKS, © ESTATE OF EDWARD BAWDEN. SOURCE – INEXPENSIVE PROGRESS.

PAGE 88 – EDWARD BAWDEN – DESIGN FOR THE ORIENT LINE, 1949, © ESTATE OF EDWARD BAWDEN. SOURCE – INEXPENSIVE PROGRESS.

PAGE 89 – EDWARD BAWDEN – LINE DRAWING FROM *LIFE IN AN ENGLISH VILLAGE*, 1949, KING PENGUIN BOOKS, © ESTATE OF EDWARD BAWDEN. SOURCE – INEXPENSIVE PROGRESS.

PAGE 91 – EDWARD BAWDEN – "A VILLAGE STORE", FROM *LIFE IN AN ENGLISH VILLAGE*, 1949, KING PENGUIN BOOKS, © ESTATE OF EDWARD BAWDEN. SOURCE – INEXPENSIVE PROGRESS.

PAGE 92 – ERIC RAVILIOUS – DESIGN FOR BOOKPLATE, 1937, G.386. SOURCE – INEXPENSIVE PROGRESS.

PAGE 93 – (TOP) EDWARD BAWDEN – ORIGINAL COLOUR DESIGN FOR "A VILLAGE STORE", FOR *LIFE IN AN ENGLISH VILLAGE*, 1949, KING PENGUIN BOOKS, FROM BRIAN WEBB AND PEYTON SKIPWITH, *EDWARD BAWDEN SCRAPBOOKS*, 2016, LUND HUMPHRIES, © ESTATE OF EDWARD BAWDEN. SOURCE – FRY ART GALLERY; (BOTTOM) EDWARD BAWDEN – DRAWING FOR THE LABOUR PARTY BOOKLET *FOOD FOR THOUGHT*, 1947, © ESTATE OF EDWARD BAWDEN. SOURCE – INEXPENSIVE PROGRESS.

PAGE 95 – EDWARD BAWDEN – "THE BAKER", FROM *LIFE IN AN ENGLISH VILLAGE*, 1949, KING PENGUIN BOOKS, © ESTATE OF EDWARD BAWDEN. SOURCE – INEXPENSIVE PROGRESS.

PAGE 96 – EDWARD BAWDEN – FRONTISPIECE FROM MAGDA JOICEY, *THE COOK-BOOK NOTE-BOOK*, 1946, WESTHOUSE BOOKS, © ESTATE OF EDWARD BAWDEN. SOURCE – INEXPENSIVE PROGRESS.

PAGE 97 – EDWARD BAWDEN – PRINTER'S PROOF OF "THE BAKER", FOR *LIFE IN AN ENGLISH VILLAGE*, 1949, KING PENGUIN BOOKS, © ESTATE OF EDWARD BAWDEN. SOURCE – INEXPENSIVE PROGRESS.

PAGE 99 – EDWARD BAWDEN – "THE BUTCHER", FROM *LIFE IN AN ENGLISH VILLAGE*, 1949, KING PENGUIN BOOKS, © ESTATE OF EDWARD BAWDEN. SOURCE – INEXPENSIVE PROGRESS.

PAGE 101 – (TOP) VINE STREET, GREAT BARDFIELD. SOURCE – STELLA HERBERT; (BOTTOM) VINE STREET, GREAT BARDFIELD, WITH A VIEW OF NORTH PLACE HOUSE. SOURCE – STELLA HERBERT.

PAGE 102 – EDWARD BAWDEN – *CATTLE MARKET, BRAINTREE*, 1937, CONTEMPORARY LITHOGRAPHS, © ESTATE OF EDWARD BAWDEN. SOURCE – FRY ART GALLERY.

PAGE 103 – EDWARD BAWDEN – *SMITHFIELD MARKET*, 1967, © ESTATE OF EDWARD BAWDEN. SOURCE – FRY ART GALLERY

PAGE 105 – EDWARD BAWDEN – "THE TAILOR", FROM *LIFE IN AN ENGLISH VILLAGE*, 1949, KING PENGUIN BOOKS, © ESTATE OF EDWARD BAWDEN. SOURCE – INEXPENSIVE PROGRESS.

PAGE 106 – *BRAINTREE AND WITHAM TIMES* - 1953. PRIVATE COLLECTION.

PAGE 107 – EDWARD BAWDEN – PRINTER'S PROOF OF "THE TAILOR", FOR *LIFE IN AN ENGLISH VILLAGE*, 1949, KING PENGUIN BOOKS, © ESTATE OF EDWARD BAWDEN. SOURCE – INEXPENSIVE PROGRESS.

PAGE 109 – EDWARD BAWDEN – "THE SADDLER'S SHOP", FROM *LIFE IN AN ENGLISH VILLAGE*, 1949, KING PENGUIN BOOKS, © ESTATE OF EDWARD BAWDEN. SOURCE – INEXPENSIVE PROGRESS.

PAGE 110 A HARNESS MAKER AT WORK IN THE VILLAGE OF GREAT BARDFIELD, 24TH NOVEMBER 1950 HULTON ARCHIVE, © GETTY IMAGES.

PAGE 111 – SOURCE – STELLA HERBERT.

PAGE 113 – EDWARD BAWDEN – "THE MARKET GARDENER", FROM *LIFE IN AN ENGLISH VILLAGE*, 1949, KING PENGUIN BOOKS, © ESTATE OF EDWARD BAWDEN. SOURCE – INEXPENSIVE PROGRESS.

PAGE 114 – EDWARD BAWDEN – DECORATION FROM *THE KYNOCH PRESS NOTE BOOK*, 1936, © ESTATE OF EDWARD BAWDEN. SOURCE – INEXPENSIVE PROGRESS.

PAGE 115 – EDWARD BAWDEN – *JUDGING THE PRIZES*, FROM *ALPHABET AND IMAGE 2*, SHENVAL PRESS, 1946, © ESTATE OF EDWARD BAWDEN. SOURCE – INEXPENSIVE PROGRESS.

PAGE 116 – EDWARD BAWDEN – DETAILS FROM PRINTER'S PROOF OF "PEELING POTATOES", FOR *LIFE IN AN ENGLISH VILLAGE*, 1949, KING PENGUIN BOOKS, © ESTATE OF EDWARD BAWDEN. SOURCE – INEXPENSIVE PROGRESS.

PAGE 118 – EDWARD BAWDEN – © ESTATE OF EDWARD BAWDEN. SOURCE – INEXPENSIVE PROGRESS.

PAGE 119 – (LEFT AND RIGHT) EDWARD BAWDEN – LINE DRAWINGS FROM *LIFE IN AN ENGLISH VILLAGE*, 1949, KING PENGUIN BOOKS, © ESTATE OF EDWARD BAWDEN. SOURCE – INEXPENSIVE PROGRESS.

PAGE 120 – (LEFT AND RIGHT) EDWARD BAWDEN – LINE DRAWINGS FROM *LIFE IN AN ENGLISH VILLAGE*, 1949, KING PENGUIN BOOKS, © ESTATE OF EDWARD BAWDEN. SOURCE – INEXPENSIVE PROGRESS.

PAGE 121 – (LEFT AND RIGHT) EDWARD BAWDEN – LINE DRAWINGS FROM *LIFE IN AN ENGLISH VILLAGE*, 1949, KING PENGUIN BOOKS, © ESTATE OF EDWARD BAWDEN. SOURCE – INEXPENSIVE PROGRESS.

PAGE 122 – TIRZAH GARWOOD – *BRICK HOUSE KITCHEN*, 1932. SOURCE – INEXPENSIVE PROGRESS.

PAGE 125 – RICHARD BAWDEN – *A SPLASH IN THE PANT*, 1992, © RICHARD BAWDEN. SOURCE – FRY ART GALLERY.

PAGE 126 – (TOP) ERIC RAVILIOUS – *HOVIS MILL*, 1935. SOURCE – INEXPENSIVE PROGRESS. (BOTTOM) THE PIPER GIRLS AT THE MILL, GREAT BARDFIELD. SOURCE – STELLA HERBERT.

PAGE 130 – THE PRODUCE SHOP, GREAT BARDFIELD. SOURCE – STELLA HERBERT.

PAGE 131 – *THE PRODUCE SHOP*, FROM *ALPHABET AND IMAGE 2*, SHENVAL PRESS, 1946, © ESTATE OF EDWARD BAWDEN. SOURCE – INEXPENSIVE PROGRESS.

PAGE 132 – EDWARD BAWDEN – LINE DRAWING FROM *LIFE IN AN ENGLISH VILLAGE*, 1949, KING PENGUIN BOOKS, © ESTATE OF EDWARD BAWDEN. SOURCE – INEXPENSIVE PROGRESS.

PAGE 133 – LUCIE ALDRIDGE'S PAIR OF SALT-GLAZED STONEWARE LIONS. SOURCE – VICTORIA AND ALBERT MUSEUM.

PAGE 134 – EDWARD BAWDEN – LINE DRAWING FROM *LIFE IN AN ENGLISH VILLAGE*, 1949, KING PENGUIN BOOKS, © ESTATE OF EDWARD BAWDEN. SOURCE – INEXPENSIVE PROGRESS.

PAGE 137 – MICHAEL ROTHENSTEIN – *BUTTERFLIES*, 1981, © ESTATE OF MICHAEL ROTHENSTEIN. SOURCE – INEXPENSIVE PROGRESS.

PAGE 138 – KENNETH ROWNTREE – *ADAM WITH PRAM*, 1943, © ESTATE OF KENNETH ROWNTREE . SOURCE – FRY ART GALLERY.

PAGE 142 – EDWARD BAWDEN – *TOWN HALL YARD*, GREAT BARDFIELD, 1956, © ESTATE OF EDWARD BAWDEN. SOURCE – FRY ART GALLERY.

PAGE 143 – (TOP) WARTIME PHOTOGRAPH OF THE CAFE, HIGH STREET, GREAT BARDFIELD. SOURCE – STELLA HERBERT; (BOTTOM) ARMISTICE DAY PHOTOGRAPH, THE TOWN HALL, GREAT BARDFIELD. SOURCE – STELLA HERBERT.

PAGE 144 – WALTER HOYLE – *GREAT BARDFIELD MILL*, 1954, © ESTATE OF WALTER HOYLE. SOURCE – INEXPENSIVE PROGRESS.

PAGE 147 – EDWARD BAWDEN – DESIGN FOR THE ORIENT LINE, 1949, © ESTATE OF EDWARD BAWDEN. SOURCE – INEXPENSIVE PROGRESS.

PAGE 149 – JOHN ALDRIDGE – *GREAT BARDFIELD*, ARTISTS' INTERNATIONAL ASSOCIATION PRINT, 1951. © ESTATE OF JOHN ALDRIDGE. SOURCE – FRY ART GALLERY.

PAGE 150 – EDWARD BAWDEN – *AUTUMN*, 1950, © ESTATE OF EDWARD BAWDEN. SOURCE – FRY ART GALLERY.

PAGE 152 – EDWARD BAWDEN – DECORATION FROM *THE KYNOCH PRESS NOTE BOOK*, 1936, © ESTATE OF EDWARD BAWDEN. SOURCE – INEXPENSIVE PROGRESS.

PAGE 153 – EDWARD BAWDEN – DECORATION FROM *THE KYNOCH PRESS NOTE BOOK*, 1936, © ESTATE OF EDWARD BAWDEN. SOURCE – INEXPENSIVE PROGRESS.

PAGE 155 – EDWARD BAWDEN – *AND THE SPIES*, ORIGINAL ARTWORK FOR THE NEW TESTAMENT, 1968, OXFORD UNIVERSITY PRESS, © ESTATE OF EDWARD BAWDEN. SOURCE – INEXPENSIVE PROGRESS.

PAGE 156 – EDWARD MORGAN – PHOTO OF EDWARD BAWDEN, © EDWARD MORGAN.

PAGE 158 – EDWARD BAWDEN – LINE DRAWING FROM *LIFE IN AN ENGLISH VILLAGE*, 1949, KING PENGUIN BOOKS, © ESTATE OF EDWARD BAWDEN. SOURCE – INEXPENSIVE PROGRESS.

PAGE 161 – PAUL NASH – WOODCUT FROM *GENESIS*, 1924, NONESUCH PRESS.

PAGE 162 – EDWARD BAWDEN – *EVELINA*, LINOCUT, © ESTATE OF EDWARD BAWDEN. SOURCE – FRY ART GALLERY

PAGE 163 – EDWARD BAWDEN – *HENRY AND ELIZA*, LINOCUT, © ESTATE OF EDWARD BAWDEN. SOURCE – FRY ART GALLERY

PAGE 164 – EDWARD BAWDEN – *JOSEPH ANDREWS AND SHAMELA* , LINOCUT, © ESTATE OF EDWARD BAWDEN. SOURCE – FRY ART GALLERY

PAGE 165 – EDWARD BAWDEN – *HUMPHRY CLINKER*, LINOCUT, © ESTATE OF EDWARD BAWDEN. SOURCE – FRY ART GALLERY

PAGE 167 – EDWARD BAWDEN – *BRIGHTON, SUBURBAN LIFE*, LINE DRAWING FROM *ALPHABET AND IMAGE 2*, SHENVAL PRESS, 1946, © ESTATE OF EDWARD BAWDEN. SOURCE – INEXPENSIVE PROGRESS.

PAGE 168 – THOMAS HENNELL – *EGDON HEATH*, 1938/9. SOURCE – INEXPENSIVE PROGRESS.

PAGE 170 – CHLOE CHEESE – *THE RADIO*, 1982, © CHLOE CHEESE. SOURCE – INEXPENSIVE PROGRESS.